First World War
and Army of Occupation
War Diary
France, Belgium and Germany

34 DIVISION
102 Infantry Brigade
Headquarters
1 January 1918 - 28 February 1918

WO95/2461/1

The Naval & Military Press Ltd
www.nmarchive.com
Published in association with The National Archives

Published by

The Naval & Military Press Ltd

Unit 10 Ridgewood Industrial Park,

Uckfield, East Sussex,

TN22 5QE England

Tel: +44 (0) 1825 749494

www.naval-military-press.com

www.nmarchive.com

This diary has been reprinted in facsimile from the original. Any imperfections are inevitably reproduced and the quality may fall short of modern type and cartographic standards.

© Crown Copyright
Images reproduced by permission of The National Archives, London, England, 2015.

Contents

Document type	Place/Title	Date From	Date To
Heading	34th Division 102nd Infy Bde Bde Headquarters 1918 Jan-1919 Jly.		
Heading	War Diary Headquarters 102nd Inf Bde. Vol 25.		
Heading	Disposition Report. 102nd Inf. Bde.		
Miscellaneous	102nd Infantry Brigade Disposition Report.	01/01/1918	01/01/1918
Miscellaneous	102nd Infantry Brigade Disposition Report.	05/01/1918	05/01/1918
Miscellaneous	102nd Infantry Brigade Disposition Report.	09/01/1918	09/01/1918
Miscellaneous	102nd Infantry Brigade Disposition Report.	13/01/1918	13/01/1918
Miscellaneous	102nd Infantry Brigade Dispositions After Relief Tomorrow, 20-1-18.	20/01/1918	20/01/1918
Miscellaneous	102nd Infantry Brigade Dispositions After Relief Tomorrow, 23-1-1918.	23/01/1918	23/01/1918
Miscellaneous	102nd Infantry Brigade Dispositions Report.	25/01/1918	25/01/1918
Miscellaneous	102nd (Tyneside Scottish) Brigade. Disposition Report.	26/01/1918	26/01/1918
Miscellaneous	Disposition Report. 102nd (Tyneside Scottish) Brigade.	29/01/1918	29/01/1918
Heading	Defence Scheme. Casualties, Honours & Awards. 102nd Inf. Bde.		
Miscellaneous	102 Infantry Brigade Defence Scheme, Centre Section, 34th Division Front. Appendix 6.	18/01/1918	18/01/1918
Miscellaneous	102 Infantry Brigade Defence Scheme, Centre Section, 34th Division Front.		
Miscellaneous	Defence Scheme Centre Section-34th Div. Front.		
Miscellaneous	Part II. General Principles Of Defence.		
Miscellaneous	Part III. Method Of Holding The Line & Allotment Of Troops.		
Miscellaneous	Action In Case Of Hostile Attack.		
Miscellaneous	Appendix 'A'.		
Miscellaneous	Appendix "B" Signal Communication.		
Miscellaneous	Appendix "C" Instructions Regarding The Sending Of The S.O.S. Message.		
Heading	Operation Orders 102nd Inf. Bde.		
Operation(al) Order(s)	102nd Infantry Brigade Order No. 181.	31/12/1917	31/12/1917
Operation(al) Order(s)	102nd Infantry Brigade Order No. 182.	08/01/1918	08/01/1918
Operation(al) Order(s)	102nd Infantry Brigade Order No. 183. Appendix 1 (C).	09/01/1918	09/01/1918
Operation(al) Order(s)	102nd Infantry Brigade Order No. 184.	13/01/1918	13/01/1918
Operation(al) Order(s)	102nd Infantry Brigade Order No. 185. Appendix I (C).	16/01/1918	16/01/1918
Operation(al) Order(s)	102nd Infantry Brigade Order No. 186. Appendix 1 (F).	17/01/1918	17/01/1918
Operation(al) Order(s)	102nd Infantry Brigade Order No. 187. Appendix 1 (g).	20/01/1918	20/01/1918
Operation(al) Order(s)	102nd Infantry Brigade Order No. 188. Appendix 1 (h).	22/01/1918	22/01/1918
Miscellaneous	T.S.48/105.	26/01/1918	26/01/1918
Operation(al) Order(s)	102nd Infantry Brigade Order No. 189. Appendix 1 (j).	23/01/1918	23/01/1918
Miscellaneous	Table "A" To accompany 102 Inf. Bde. Order No. 189.		
Heading	Daily Intelligence Summaries 102nd Inf. Bde. Appendix 2.		
War Diary	N.22.d.4.4 Sheet 51 B.S.W.	01/01/1918	27/01/1918
War Diary	M.3.b.c.8.0.	28/01/1918	30/01/1918
Miscellaneous	Casualties January 1918. Officers. Nil. Other Ranks. Appendix 4.		
Miscellaneous	List Of Honours And Awards-January 1918. Appendix 5.		

Miscellaneous	Intelligence Summary 102nd (Tyneside Scottish) Brigade.	31/12/1917	31/12/1917
Miscellaneous	Patrols.	01/01/1918	01/01/1918
Miscellaneous	Intelligence Summary 102nd (Tyneside Scottish) Bde.	01/01/1918	01/01/1918
Miscellaneous	To accompany Intell. G.31 Patrols.	02/01/1918	02/01/1918
Miscellaneous	102nd (Tyneside Scottish) Bde. Intelligence Summary.	02/01/1918	02/01/1918
Miscellaneous	Intelligence Summary 102nd (Tyneside Scottish) Brigade.	03/01/1918	03/01/1918
Miscellaneous	Patrols.	04/01/1918	04/01/1918
Miscellaneous	Intelligence Summary 102nd (Tyneside Scottish) Brigade.	04/01/1918	04/01/1918
Miscellaneous	Intelligence Summary 102nd (Tyneside Scottish) Brigade.	05/01/1918	05/01/1918
Miscellaneous	Intelligence Summary 102nd (Tyneside Scottish) Brigade.	06/01/1918	06/01/1918
Miscellaneous	To accompany Intell. G. 55.	07/01/1918	07/01/1918
Miscellaneous	Intelligence Summary 102nd (Tyneside Scottish) Brigade.	07/01/1918	07/01/1918
Miscellaneous	Intelligence Summary 102nd (Tyneside Scottish) Brigade.	08/01/1918	08/01/1918
Miscellaneous	Intelligence Summary 102nd (Tyneside Scottish) Brigade.	09/01/1918	09/01/1918
Miscellaneous	Intelligence Summary 102nd (Tyneside Scottish) Brigade.	10/01/1918	10/01/1918
Miscellaneous	Intelligence Summary 102nd (Tyneside Scottish) Brigade.	12/01/1918	12/01/1918
Miscellaneous	Intelligence Summary 102nd (Tyneside Scottish) Brigade.	13/01/1918	13/01/1918
Miscellaneous	Intelligence Summary 102nd (Tyneside Scottish) Brigade.	14/01/1918	14/01/1918
Miscellaneous	Intelligence Summary 102nd (Tyneside Scottish) Brigade.	15/01/1918	15/01/1918
Miscellaneous	Intelligence Summary 102nd (Tyneside Scottish) Brigade.	16/01/1918	16/01/1918
Miscellaneous	Intelligence Summary 102nd (Tyneside Scottish) Brigade.	17/01/1918	17/01/1918
Miscellaneous	Intelligence Summary 102nd (Tyneside Scottish) Brigade.	18/01/1918	18/01/1918
Miscellaneous	Intelligence Summary 102nd (Tyneside Scottish) Brigade.	19/01/1918	19/01/1918
Miscellaneous	Intelligence Summary 102nd (Tyneside Scottish) Brigade.	20/01/1918	20/01/1918
Miscellaneous	Intelligence Summary 102nd (Tyneside Scottish) Brigade.	21/01/1918	21/01/1918
Miscellaneous	Patrols.	22/01/1918	22/01/1918
Miscellaneous	Intelligence Summary 102nd (Tyneside Scottish) Brigade.	22/01/1918	22/01/1918
Miscellaneous	Patrols.	23/01/1918	23/01/1918
Miscellaneous	Intelligence Summary 102nd (Tyneside Scottish) Brigade.	23/01/1918	23/01/1918
Miscellaneous	Intelligence Summary 102nd (T.S.) Brigade.	24/01/1918	24/01/1918
Miscellaneous	Intelligence Summary 102nd (Tyneside Scottish) Brigade.	25/01/1918	25/01/1918
Heading	War Diary H.Q. 102. Infantry. Bde. February 1918. Vol 26.		
War Diary	M.36.c.8.0. Sheet 51 B. S.W.	01/02/1918	07/02/1918

War Diary	Blaireville.	09/02/1918	09/02/1918
War Diary	Gouy-En-Artois.	10/02/1918	10/02/1918
War Diary	Ambrines.	11/02/1918	27/02/1918
War Diary	Pommier.	28/02/1918	28/02/1918
Miscellaneous	Casualties. February 1918. Officers. Nil. Appendix 3.		
Heading	Honours And Awards. February 1918. Nil. Appendix 4.		
Heading	Operation Orders. Appendix 1.		
Operation(al) Order(s)	102nd Infantry Brigade Order No. 181. Appendix 1 (b).	26/02/1918	26/02/1918
Miscellaneous	March On Feb. 27th. 1918 Table A. To accompany O.O. No. 191.		
Operation(al) Order(s)	Addressed all Recipients of O.O. 191.	27/02/1918	27/02/1918
Miscellaneous	Ref. Map. Sheet 11 Lens. Table B March On Feb. 28th 1918. To accompany O.O. 191.	28/02/1918	28/02/1918
Operation(al) Order(s)	102nd Infantry Brigade Order No. 190. Appendix 1 (a).	07/02/1918	07/02/1918
Miscellaneous	Table "A" March On Feb. 9th 1918.	09/02/1918	09/02/1918
Miscellaneous	Table "B" March On Feb. 10th 1918. To accompany 102nd Bde. Order No. 190.	10/02/1918	10/02/1918
Miscellaneous	Table 'C' March On Feb 11th 1918 To accompany 102nd Bde. Order No. 190.	11/02/1918	11/02/1918
Miscellaneous	Administrative Instructions No. 12.	02/02/1918	02/02/1918
Miscellaneous	Table "A".		
Miscellaneous	Table "B" Postions of officers of 20th and 21st Bns. Northd. Fusiliers.		
Miscellaneous	Table "C" Table Of Moves.		
Miscellaneous	Appendix 2 will be issued later.	19/02/1918	19/02/1918
Miscellaneous	Preparatory Orders for move by train while in G.H.Q. reserve.	19/02/1918	19/02/1918
Miscellaneous	Appendix 1. Instructions for move by strategical Train.		
Miscellaneous	Table A-Entrainment by Strategical Train.		
Miscellaneous	Appendix 2. Move by Tactical Train.		
Miscellaneous	Table B-Entrainment by Tactical Train.		
Miscellaneous	Administrative Instructions No. 13.	07/02/1918	07/02/1918
Miscellaneous	Table "A"-Allotment Of Lorries.		
Heading	Disposition. Reports. Appendix 2.		
Miscellaneous	Dispositions Report.	10/02/1918	10/02/1918
Miscellaneous	102 Brigade Group Dispositions after March tomorrow, Feb. 9th.	08/02/1918	08/02/1918
Miscellaneous	Dispositions After Moves To-Day.	03/02/1918	03/02/1918

34TH DIVISION
102ND INFY BDE

BDE HEADQUARTERS

1918 JAN - ~~DEC 1918~~ 1917 JLY

28031 W3125/M2250 1000m 6/17 M.R.Co.,Ltd. (1367) Forms W3091.   Army Form W. 3091.

Vol 25
January 1918.

Cover for Documents.

Nature of Enclosures.

WAR DIARY,

HEADQUARTERS,

102ND INF BDE.

Notes, or Letters written.

28031 W3125/M2250 1000m 6/17 M.R.Co.,Ltd. (1367) Forms W3091.   Army Form W. 3091.

Cover for Documents.

Natures of Enclosures.

Appendix 3.

DISPOSITION
REPORTS

102ND INF. BDE.

Notes, or Letters written.

SECRET

"War Diary"

Headquarters,
34th Division.

T.S.21/22

102nd INFANTRY BRIGADE
DISPOSITION REPORT.

	Location 1-1-1918	Location after relief 2-1-17
BRIGADE HEADQUARTERS	N.22.d.4.4.	N.22.d.4.4.
20th Northd. Fusiliers (1st TYNESIDE SCOTTISH)	N.35.c.45.30.	O.25.c.05.45.
21st Northd. Fusiliers (2nd TYNESIDE SCOTTISH)	N.30.a.3.3.	N.36.b.3.1.
22nd Northd. Fusiliers (3rd TYNESIDE SCOTTISH)	O.25.c.05.45.	N.35.c.45.30.
23rd Northd. Fusiliers (4th TYNESIDE SCOTTISH)	N.36.b.3.1.	N.30.a.3.3.
102 Machine Gun Coy.	N.35.c.1.8.	N.35.c.1.8.
102 Light T.M. Bty.	N.29.b.2.8.	N.29.b.2.8.

102 B.H.Q.
1-1-1918.

LIEUTENANT COLONEL,
COMMDG. 102nd (TYNESIDE SCOTTISH) BDE.

SECRET

War Copy

T.S.21/75

Headquarters,
34th Division.

102nd INFANTRY BRIGADE
DISPOSITION REPORT

	Location 5-1-1918	Location after relief 6-1-18
BRIGADE HEADQUARTERS	N.22.d.4.4.	N.22.d.4.4.
20th Northd. Fusiliers. (1st TYNESIDE SCOTTISH)	O.25.c.05.45.	N.30.a.3.3.
21st Northd. Fusiliers. (2nd TYNESIDE SCOTTISH)	N36.b.3.1.	N.35.c.45.30.
22nd Northd. Fusiliers. (3rd TYNESIDE SCOTTISH)	N.35.c.45.30.	O.25.c.05.45.
23rd Northd. Fusiliers. (4th TYNESIDE SCOTTISH)	N.30.a.3.3.	N.36.b.3.1.
102 Machine Gun Coy.	N.35.c.1.8.	N.35.c.1.8.
102 Light T.M. Bty.	N.29.b.2.8.	N.29.b.2.8.

102 B.H.Q.
5-1-1918.

LIEUTENANT COLONEL.
COMMDG. 102nd (TYNESIDE SCOTTISH) BDE.

SECRET

Headquarters,
34th Division.

102nd INFANTRY BRIGADE DISPOSITION REPORT

	Location 9-1-1918	Location aft relief 10-1-
BRIGADE HEADQUARTERS	N.22.d.4.4.	N.22.d.4.4.
20th Northd. Fusiliers (1st TYNESIDE SCOTTISH)	N.30.a.3.3.	O.25.c.05.45.
21st Northd. Fusiliers (2nd TYNESIDE SCOTTISH)	N.35.c.45.30.	N.36.b.3.1.
22nd Northd. Fusiliers (3rd TYNESIDE SCOTTISH)	O.25.c.05.45.	N.30.a.3.3.
23rd Northd. Fusiliers (4th TYNESIDE SCOTTISH)	N.36.b.3.1.	N.35.c.45.30.
102 Machine Gun Company	N.35.c.1.8.	N.35.c.1.8.
102 Light T.M. Bty.	N.29.b.2.8.	N.29.b.2.8.

102 B.H.Q.
9-1-1918

LIEUTENANT COLONEL.
COMMDG. 102nd (TYNESIDE SCOTTISH) BDE.

SECRET   T.S.21/30

War Diary

Headquarters,
34th Division.

102nd INFANTRY BRIGADE DISPOSITION REPORT

	Location 13-1-1918	Location after relief 14-1-18.
BRIGADE HEADQUARTERS	N.22.d.4.4.	N.22.d.4.4.
20th Northd. Fusiliers (1st TYNESIDE SCOTTISH)	O.25.c.05.45.	N.35.c.45.30.
21st Northd. Fusiliers (2nd TYNESIDE SCOTTISH)	N.36.b.3.1.	N.30.a.3.3.
22nd Northd. Fusiliers (3rd TYNESIDE SCOTTISH)	N.30.a.3.3.	O.25.c.05.45.
23rd Northd. Fusiliers (4th TYNESIDE SCOTTISH)	N.35.c.45.30.	N.36.b.3.1.
102 Machine Gun Coy.	N.35.c.1.8.	N.35.c.1.8.
102 Light T.M. Bty.	T.5.a.8.6.	T.5.a.8.6.

102 B.H.Q.
13-1-1918.

for LIEUTENANT COLONEL.
COMMDG. 102nd (TYNESIDE SCOTTISH) BDE.

SECRET   WAR DIARY   T.S.21/33

Headquarters,
34th Division.

102nd INFANTRY BRIGADE
DISPOSITIONS AFTER RELIEF TOMORROW, 20-1-18

BRIGADE HEADQUARTERS .... M.22.d.4.4.

20th Northd. Fusiliers ...... M.30.a.3.3.

21st Northd. Fusiliers ...... M.35.c.45.30.

22nd Northd. Fusiliers ...... O.25.c.05.45.

23rd Northd. Fusiliers ...... M.33.b.3.1.

102 Machine Gun Coy. .... HENIN CAMP
103 Machine Gun Coy   N.35.c.1.8.
102 Light T.M. Bty. .... T.5.a.8.6.

102 B.H.Q.
19-1-18.   LIEUTENANT COLONEL
               COMMDG. 102nd (TYNESIDE SCOTTISH) BRIGADE.

SECRET

WAR DIARY T.S.21/35

Headquarters,
34th Division.

102nd INFANTRY BRIGADE
DISPOSITIONS AFTER RELIEF TOMORROW, 23-1-1918

BRIGADE HEADQUARTERS	N.22.d.4.4.
20th Northd. Fusiliers. (1st TYNESIDE SCOTTISH).	~~N.36.b.5.1.~~ O 25 c 05 45
21st Northd. Fusiliers (2nd TYNESIDE SCOTTISH)	N.36.b.3.1.
22nd Northd. Fusiliers (3rd TYNESIDE SCOTTISH)	N.30.a.3.3.
23rd Northd. Fusiliers (4th TYNESIDE SCOTTISH)	N.35.c.45.30.
102 Machine Gun Coy.	HENIN CAMP
103 Machine Gun Coy.	N.35.a.1.8.
102 Light T.M. Battery	T.5.a.8.6.

22-1-1918

BRIGADIER GENERAL.
COMMDG. 102nd (TYNESIDE SCOTTISH) BRIGADE.

SECRET

Headquarters,
34th Division.

102nd INFANTRY BRIGADE
DISPOSITION REPORT
After relief today Jan. 25th.

BRIGADE HEADQUARTERS .... N.22.d.4.4.

20th Northd. Fusiliers
(1st TYNESIDE SCOTTISH) .... O.25.c.05.45.

21st Northd. Fusiliers.
(2nd TYNESIDE SCOTTISH) .... N.36.b.3.1.

22nd Northd. Fusiliers
(3rd TYNESIDE SCOTTISH) .... NORTHUMBERLAND LINES.

23rd Northd. Fusiliers.
(4th TYNESIDE SCOTTISH) .... YORK LINES

1st Northd. Fusiliers. .... N.30.a.3.3.

4th Royal Fusiliers .... N.35.c.45.30.

102 L.T.M.B. .... T.5.a.8.6.

103 M.G. Coy. .... N.35.c.1.8.

25-1-1918.   BRIGADIER GENERAL.
                COMMDG. 102nd (TYNESIDE SCOTTISH) BDE.

SECRET

Headquarters,
    34th Division.

102nd (TYNESIDE SCOTTISH) BRIGADE.

DISPOSITION REPORT

(a) After relief tonight

BRIGADE HEADQUARTERS	N.22.d.4.4.
20th Northd. Fusiliers	N.30.a.3.3.
21st Northd. Fusiliers	N.35.c.45.30.
22nd Northd. Fusiliers	NORTHUMBERLAND LINES.
23rd Northd. Fusiliers	YORK LINES
1st Northd. Fusiliers	O.25.c.05.45.
4th Royal Fusiliers	N.36.b.3.1.
102 Light T.M. Bty.	T.5.a.8.6.

(b) After relief tomorrow night.

BRIGADE HEADQUARTERS	N.36.c.8.0.
20th Northd. Fusiliers	DURHAM LINES A
21st Northd. Fusiliers	DURHAM LINES B
22nd Northd. Fusiliers	NORTHUMBERLAND LINES
23rd Northd. Fusiliers	YORK LINES
102 Light T.M. Bty.	YORK LINES

102 B.H.Q.
26-1-1918

BRIGADIER GENERAL
COMMDG. 102nd (TYNESIDE SCOTTISH) BDE.

SECRET

T.S.21/42

Headquarters,
34th Division
--

DISPOSITION REPORT
102nd (TYNESIDE SCOTTISH) BRIGADE.

BRIGADE HEADQUARTERS .... M.36.c.8.0.

20th Northd. Fusiliers
(1st TYNESIDE SCOTTISH) .... DURHAM LINES A

21st Northd. Fusiliers
(2nd TYNESIDE SCOTTISH) .... DURHAM LINES B

22nd Northd. Fusiliers
(3rd TYNESIDE SCOTTISH) ...... NORTHUMBERLAND LINES.

23rd Northd. Fusiliers
(4TH TYNESIDE SCOTTISH) ...... YORK LINES

102 Machine Gun Company ...... B.21.a.8.7.

102 Light T.M. Battery .... YORK LINES

102 B.H.Q.
29-1-1918

BRIGADIER GENERAL
COMMDG. 102nd (TYNESIDE SCOTTISH) BDE.

28031 W3125/M2250 1000m 6/17 M.R.Co.,Ltd. (1367) Forms W3091. Army Form W. 3091.

Cover for Documents.

Natures of Enclosures.

DEFENCE SCHEME,
CASUALTIES,
HONOURS
&
AWARDS.

102ND INF. BDE.

Notes, or Letters written.

WAR DIARY Appendix 6

SECRET

Copy No ... 16

102 INFANTRY BRIGADE DEFENCE SCHEME, CENTRE SECTION, 34th DIVISION FRONT.

Issued January 18th 1918.

Distribution

G.O.C.	Copy No. 1
Brigade Major	" " 2
Staff Captain	" " 3
Brigade Signal Officer	" " 4
Right Battalion	" " 5
Left Battalion	" " 6
Support Battalion	" " 7
Reserve Battalion	" " 8
Machine Gun Company	" " 9
Light Trench Mortar Battery	" " 10
Centre Group, R.F.A.	" " 11
Field Company, R.E.	" " 12
34th Division	" " 13
Right Infantry Brigade	" " 14
Left Infantry Brigade	" " 15

102 B.H.Q.

Tribridge
Major.
BRIGADE MAJOR.
102nnd (TYNESIDE SCOTTISH) BRIGADE.

102 INFANTRY BRIGADE DEFENCE SCHEME, CENTRE SECTION, 34th DIVISION FRONT

CONTENTS

Part I — Frontage and organisation of 34th Div. Area.
Defensive organisation.
Tactical features in Centre Section.

Part II — General Principles of Defence.
Functions of Lines of Defence in Forward Zone.
Machine Gun Defence in Forward Zone.

Part III — Method of holding the Line and Allotment of Troops.

Part IV — Action in case of hostile attack.
Readiness of Reserve and Support Battalions.

APPENDICES

- **A** — Artillery S.O.S. Lines.
  Concentrations to deal with local attacks.
  Artillery Support from Right & Left Groups, R.F.A.
  Counter Preparation Schemes 'A', 'B' and 'C'.
- **B** — Signal Communications.
- **C** — Instructions regarding the sending of the S.O.S. message.
- **D** — Administrative Instructions.

MAPS

- **A** — Trenches of Forward Zone, First and Second Battle systems.
  Boundaries of Centre Section.
  Dispositions of Infantry Battalions.
- **B** — Machine gun and Stokes mortar emplacements.
  Normal S.O.S. Lines of Centre Group, R.F.A., Stokes mortars and heavy trench mortars.
  S.O.S. & Battle Lines of Machine guns.
- **C** — Signal Communications.
- **D** — Administrative.

SECRET.
Page .. 1

DEFENCE SCHEME.

CENTRE SECTION --- 34th DIV. front.

PART I.

.. Frontage and Organization of 34th Div. Area.

(a) Extent of Divisional front -
The 34th Divisional Front extends from U.14.a.00.35. across the SENSEE and COJEUL Valleys to O.14.a.70.70.

(b) Organization of Divisional front -
The Divisional Front is organized in 3 Sections each held by 1 Infantry Brigade.

(c) Boundaries of Centre Section -
The Southern boundary of the Centre Section is a line from the junction of BROWN SUPPORT and SHAFT AVENUE (T.6.a.57.85.) through U.1.a.3.7. to U.1.b.5.5.

The Northern boundary of the Centre Section is a line along SHARK AVENUE (inclusive to Centre Section) from its junction with EGRET TRENCH to point O.25.b.45.30 - thence to front line at O.26.a.45.55.

.. Defensive Organization -

(a) The defences in the Divisional Area are organized into -

(i) a Forward Zone consisting of the front, support and reserve line trenches.

(ii) a Battle Zone consisting of the first, second and third battle systems with switches between them.

(b) In the Centre Section the First Battle System consists of the trenches previously known as the Intermediate Line.

(c) The Second Battle system is a line of defence previously known as the Corps Line running approximately North and South just West of HENINEL.

(d) The HENINEL Switch joins the First Battle System to the Second Battle System in rear of the Centre Section 34th Div. front.

(e) The trenches of the Forward Zone, the First and Second Battle Systems and the HENINEL Switch are shown on Map 'A' attached.

(f) In the Centre Section the trenches of the Forward Zone are completed, those of the First Battle System are almost completed. The remaining systems of defence in rear and Switch lines have been sited and are now in course of construction.

.. Tactical features in the Centre Section -
The most important tactical feature in the Divisional Area is the high ground between CROISELLES and HENINEL known as HENIN HILL. This is the key to the whole of the Battle Zone in the Divisional Area

SECRET.
/ Part II -

Page .. 2

PART II.

GENERAL PRINCIPLES OF DEFENCE.

1.. The policy to be adopted for the defence of the front is -

    (a) to impair the enemy's fighting power by local offensives, raids, active patrolling, organized bombardments and gas discharges.

    (b) To strengthen the defences so as to be able to defeat a strong and sustained hostile offensive.

    (c) to organise the infantry, machine guns, trench mortars and artillery allotted for the defence of the line in depth.

2.. As regards para. 1 (b) it is of the greatest importance to develop the wire entanglements to the fullest extent possible to enable the forward trenches to be held lightly and so free men for reserves, minor offensive enterprises and upkeep of defences.

3.. As regards para. 1 (c) -

    (a) Battalions and smaller formations will all be disposed in depth. If any body of troops is sent forward to reinforce or counter attack, its place is to be taken immediately by other troops from the rear. This will call for the closest liaison between *Battalion and Company Commanders.*

    (b) the front line will be held as lightly as is consistent with safety. To permit of this full use must be made of Lewis Guns; the positions from which they are to fire must be selected as far as possible so as to be mutually supporting.
    By day the enemy's lines must be watched continuously by sentries and by night by frequent patrols. If this is done efficiently the enemy cannot effect a surprise.

4.. **Functions of the lines of defence in the Forward Zone** -

  (a) The functions of the front and support lines are -

    (i) to defeat minor enterprises.

    (ii) to delay a serious attack long enough to allow of the Reserve Line being manned as the main line of resistance.

  The troops in occupation of the Front and Support Lines will therefore be divided into -

    (i) fixed garrisons of posts in both lines.

    (ii) immediate counter attack troops in the Support Line to recapture lost posts or reinforce posts hard pressed in the front line.

  (b) The functions of the Reserve Line are -

    (i) to enable the front and support lines to prolong their resistance.

4.. **Functions of the lines of defence in the Forward Zone** - (contd.)

    (b) - contd -

        (ii) to form the main line of resistance in the Forward Zone.

        Troops in the Reserve Line are therefore divided into -

        (i) reinforcements for Front and Support Lines.
        (ii) fixed garrisons for the Reserve Line.

5.. **Machine Gun Defence of Forward Zone** -

    (a) The machine guns are distributed in depth and sited to form as far as possible impassable belts of fire with the object of breaking up the enemy attack and preparing the way for counter attack. They form the backbone of the infantry defence.

    (b) The functions of the machine guns in the defence are -

        (i) to put down an S.O.S. or outer screen of fire to cover the most important lines of hostile approach in No Man's Land or the enemy's front system of trenches. The line of fire for this screen will be known as the S.O.S. Line.

        (ii) if the enemy succeeds in penetrating our front and support lines, to put down an inner screen of direct fire to protect the lines of defence in rear. The line of fire for this screen will be known as the 'Battle Line'.

(/ Part III

Page .. 4

PART III

METHOD OF HOLDING THE LINE & ALLOTMENT OF TROOPS -

Infantry Battalions.

1.. The Centre Section 34th Div. front is held by one Infantry Brigade supported by the Centre Group R.F.A.

2.. Two battalions are allotted for the defence of the Front and Support lines.

Dividing line between the two forward battalions -

O. 31. b. 75. 23 -- O. 31. b. 4. 3.

Each forward battalion has 3 Companies in the front and support lines and one Company in local reserve, accommodated for convenience in the reserve line.
(This distribution is for battalions with a trench strength of 500).

3.. One battalion, called "battalion in Support" is accommodated -

1 Company in CONCRETE RESERVE.
1 Company in CUCKOO RESERVE.
1 Company in EGRET LOOP.
1 Company in CUCKOO COURT and Sunken Road O.25.o.25.55, EGRET TRENCH the WEST.

4.. One battalion is in Brigade Reserve and is accommodated in deep dugouts in SHAFT AVENUE in N.35.c. and N.34.b.

5.. For dispositions see Map 'A'.

Machine Guns.

6.. All 16 guns of the Brigade Machine Gun Company are in emplacements in and East of the first Battle system. For positions of emplacements see Map "B".

Stokes Mortars.

7.. 6 mortars are in defensive emplacements in or close in rear of the Support Line.
Mortars as required are taken to more forward positions for shoots on the enemy's trenches.

2 mortars are in Reserve.

For positions of emplacements see Map "B".

Artillery.

8.. The Centre Group R.F.A. at present comprises -

152nd Bde. R.F.A. ~~plus~~

Heavy Trench Mortars.

9.. The following trench mortars are at present in emplacements in Centre Section -

1 9.45" M K III   8 6" Newton.
1 9.45" M K I   6 2" Medium Mortars.

50% of the available 6" Newton mortars are to be moved back shortly to positions for the defence of the First Battle System.

/ Part IV

PART IV.

ACTION IN CASE OF HOSTILE ATTACK.

Front line Battalions.

1. The fixed garrisons of every post will offer the greatest resistance to the enemy of which they are capable.

2. Should the enemy penetrate any portion of our lines he is to be driven out by an immediate counter attack to be made by any Commander on the spot on his own initiative with the local reserves at his disposal at the time.

    It must be thoroughly impressed on all leaders that the counter attack, to be successful, must be delivered whilst the enemy is still disorganized and before he has had time to consolidate.

    Plans for these local counter attacks must be prepared beforehand and all leaders must thoroughly understand exactly what they are expected to do in this connection.

    To enable counter attacks to be delievered rapidly, means of exit must be provided in all trenches and troops must be practiced at night in moving over the open on ground over which they may have to counter attack.

3. The capture of a portion of our lines by the enemy is not to entail retirement elsewhere.

    Troops on the flanks of the breach will hold their ground and support the local counter attacks made by the reserves by the fire of all their weapons.

Battalion in Support.

4. The Battalion in Support will hold its present positions with the following exceptions :-

    (a) the platoon at the NEST will be moved into EGRET Trench at once.

    (b) when the Company of the Right Battalion in local reserve moves forward, the Company of the Battalion in Support in CUCKOO RESERVE will extend to the right and hold the firebays in CUCKOO PASSAGE with 1 platoon. This Company and the Company of the Battalion in Support in CONCRETE RESERVE will each establish posts of Rifle Grenadiers covering FIRST AVENUE.

    (c) when the Company of the Left Battalion in local reserve moves forward the Company of the Battalion in Support in EGRET Trench, CUCKOO COURT and the Sunken Road about O.25.c.25.55. will at once move up and occupy its place in MALLARD RESERVE.

Battalion in Brigade Reserve.

5. The Battalion in Brigade Reserve will at once assemble in and hold the First Battle system as follows :-

    1 Company -
    1 platoon in SHAFT AVENUE manning firebays South of GREY STREET to fire H.E. in front of GREY STREET and finding a Section of Rifle Grenadiers at the junction of SHAFT AVENUE and FOOLEY LANE who will keep touch with the Brigade on our Right whose left in the First Battle system rests on FOOLEY LANE.

    1 platoon in GREY STREET between junction with SHAFT AV. and point T.35.c.8.7.

    2 platoons in Support in SHAFT AVENUE just North of GREY STREET.

/ 1 Company

Battalion 5.. (continued)
in
Brigade   1 Company -
Reserve.   2 platoons in GREY STREET between N.35.c.8.7. and
N.35.c.40.55.

      2 platoons in FIRST AVENUE and BOOTHAM TRENCH between
N.35.b.9.7. and N.30.c.4.0.

1 Company - in BOOTHAM TRENCH between N.30.c.4.0. and
FOSTER AVENUE exclusive.

1 Company - will move to a position of readiness at or
South of the junction of FIRST and SUSSEX Avenues according
as hostile shelling permits so as to be able either to
reinforce the Intermediate Line or occupy selected localities
in the HENINEL Switch. The Company Commander will report
his arrival at this position and all further moves to O.C.
Support Battalion at the NEST and to Brigade Headquarters.
This Company will not move from its position of readiness
without orders from Brigade Headquarters except in case of
great emergency.
The Company Commander will establish a runner post at the
Visual Signalling Station at N.35.a.9.5. as well as at the
NEST.

The most suitable localities for defence in the HENINEL
  Switch North of the junction of FIRST and SUSSEX Avenues
  are :-

  (a) Small work at E. corner of CEMETERY at N.29.a.95.38.
      (Provides a good field of fire N.E., E. and S.E.).

  (b) Shell hole post immediately North of the Road about
      N.29.a.95.80. (Commands portion of slope not visible
      from posts (a)).

  (c) Shell hole posts astride COJEUL RIVER.
      (To command COJEUL Valley and S. exits from WANCOURT).

  (d) Shell hole post at N.22.d.60.70.
      (To command S.W. exits from WANCOURT).

  (e) Work at N.22.b.12.02.

* (f) Work at Cross Roads N.22.a.75.40.

* (g) Shell hole post immediately N. of Bank about
      N.22.b.10.50.

        * To command W. exits of WANCOURT.

Flank 6. (a) O.C. Battalion in Brigade Reserve will be prepared at
Defence.   all times to send forward 1 or 2 Companies as may be
        ordered from Brigade Headquarters to hold BROWN SUPPORT
        Trench as a defensive flank facing S.E.

Flank Defences.

6.. (continued) -

(b) In the event of a break in the line on the front of the Brigade on our left, the garrison of MALLARD RESERVE (whether found from the Left Battalion or Support Battalion at the time), will at once move 1 platoon into SHAWK AVENUE to man the firebays just West of MALLARD RESERVE to form a defensive flank facing North.

The Company in EGRET LOOP will at the same time move 1 platoon into SHAWK AVENUE to man the firebays facing North which are being constructed just East of EGRET LOOP

Readiness of Support & Reserve Battalions.

6(*).. On all occasions when either inter-Brigade or Battalion reliefs are carried out, every Company of the Battalion moving into Support will stand-to in its allotted Battle position immediately on arrival in the Support Area.

This Battalion will also stand-to daily one hour before dawn.

O.C's Support and Reserve Battalions will ensure that all their Officers are fully acquainted with the details of the action to be taken in case of attack as laid down in paras. 4, 5 and 6. - It is essential that all Company and Platoon Commanders of those Battalions should have previously reconnoitred and arranged their dispositions in each of the localities which they might be called upon to garrison in accordance with the above paras.

/ WORKING PARTIES -- 7

Page .. 7

WORKING PARTIES.

7.. (a) **Infantry** -

When there are indications that a hostile attack is imminent, all working parties and parties working in deep dugouts in and East of the Support Line, will report at once to the nearest Company Headquarters and will come under the orders of the O.C. Company concerned.

O.C's Battalions will be responsible for warning all men working in deep dugouts in their areas.

The same will apply to parties working in the Reserve Line except that they will report to and come under the orders of the O.C. nearest Battalion in the line.

Working parties in the First Battle system from the battalion in Brigade Reserve will be moved under orders of O.C. Battalion in Brigade Reserve to their allotted positions in the first Battle system.

Those of other units will hold the ground where they are at the time and report their strength and position to O.C. Battalion in Brigade Reserve under whose orders they will then come.

(b) **R.E. and Pioneers** -

The orders in para. 7 (a) will apply. When it is considered possible to do so the above will be withdrawn under orders from Brigade Headquarters and sent to their own lines.

Action of Machine Guns.

8.. (a) All machine guns will open fire on their S.O.S. lines whenever the S.O.S. signal is sent up on or near the Brigade front, whenever the enemy places a heavy barrage on our front trenches or when the enemy is known to be advancing to the attack.

In the event of a heavy local bombardment of part of the Brigade front, those machine guns whose S.O.S. lines are in the direction of the threatened area will open fire on their S.O.S. lines.

Fire will be continued on S.O.S. lines until the situation becomes quiet or until the enemy is known to have broken through our front trenches, but seven full belts will always be kept ready for fire on the Battle Line.

(b) Machine Guns will fire on their Battle Lines as soon as it is known that the enemy has broken through our front trenches.

In this case it is the duty of each gun to prevent all enemy approaching or crossing their Battle lines.

(c) Every machine gun will be fought to the last man and to the last round of ammunition. In no circumstances will any machine gun fall back.

(d) S.O.S. and Battle lines of machine guns, Centre Section, are shown on Map "B".

Action of Stokes Mortars.

9.. (a) All Stokes Mortars in positions from which fire can be brought to bear on No Man's Land will open on their S.O.S. lines at their highest rate of fire whenever the enemy places a heavy barrage on our front trenches, whenever the S.O.S. signal is sent up on the Brigade front or when the enemy is known to be advancing to the attack.

In case of a heavy local bombardment of our front trenches those mortars whose S.O.S. lines are in the direction of the threatened area will open fire

All

Page .. 8

Action 9.. (continued) -
of
Stokes
Mortars.

    (b)   All Stokes Mortars will be fought until it is evident that their capture is unavoidable when they will be destroyed.

    (c)   The Commanders of all Stokes Mortar Detachments must keep in touch with the situation in their neighbourhood. They must be continually on the lookout for opportunities of supporting our local counter attacks by their fire.

    (d)   S.O.S. lines of Stokes Mortars are shown on Map "B".

Action 10.. (a)   Normal S.O.S. lines for Centre Group R.F.A. and Heavy T.M's covering Centre Section are given in Appendix "A" and are shown on Map "B".
of
Artillery
&
Heavy T.M's.

    (b)   In the event of a general attack on the whole Divisional front all 18-pdrs. open a shrapnel barrage on their normal S.O.S. lines as close to our front trenches as safety permits.

    4.5" Hows. and Heavy T.M's fire on their normal S.O.S. lines -

    Rates of fire - (rounds per gun per minute).

	18-pdrs.	4.5" Hows.
First 5 minutes	3	2
Second 5 minutes	2	2
Third 5 minutes	1	1

    (c)   Concentrations of artillery fire have been arranged will be carried out in the event of a portion only of the front of the Centre Section being attacked. For details see Appendix 'A'.

    All Officers must understand that these concentrations can be ordered only when it is definitely known that the hostile attack is limited to a portion of our front. It is therefore of extreme importance for the situation on the whole of the Brigade front to be reported at once to Brigade Headquarters whenever anything untoward occurs even on a portion of the front only.

    (d)   In the event of the Centre Section being attacked but there being no attack on the front of the Right or Left Sections, artillery support on the front of the Centre Section will be given by the Right or Left Groups R.F.A. respectively as the case may be. For details see Appendix "A".

    (e)   In the event of a heavy hostile bombardment of our front system of trenches thought to be preparatory to a hostile attack, counter preparation bombardments will be carried out by the Div. Artillery on the enemy's trenches. For details see Appendix 'A'.

Action in 11.   Troops will act as laid down in S.S. 193.
case of   All 4.5" Hows. will fire on that portion of the enemys
hostile   trenches from which the gas is being released.
gas
cloud   Rate of fire 2 rounds. per How. per minute.
Attack.

Page .. 9

APPENDIX 'A'.

ARTILLERY ARRANGEMENTS -

(a) Normal S.O.S. Lines -

Centre Group, R.F.A.

A/152	U.1.b.25.35.	- U.1.b.60.38.
B/152	O.32.a.13.48.	- O.32.a.20.95.
C/152	O.26.c.30.32.	- O.23.c.45.80.
D/152	U.1.b.95.75.	
	O.32.c.55.32.	
	O.32.a.32.64.	
	O.26.b.20.00.	
	O.26.c.50.05.	
	O.26.c.78.67.	

Heavy Trench Mortars

9.45" mortars - O.32.b.50.95. and O.32.b.02.08.
3" Stokes ... - O.26.b.6.6.
O.26.d.5.3.
O.26.c.50.32.
O.32.c.2.3.
U.1.b.7.6

(b) S.O.S. FONTAINE -
This concentration will be ordered in the event of a hostile attack limited to the Right Battalion front -

A/152	3 guns	U.1.a.32.60.	- U.1.b.67.63.
	3 guns	U.1.b.67.63.	- U.1.b.78.87.
B/152	6 guns	U.1.b.78.87.	- O.32.c.08.27.
C/152	3 guns	O.32.c.08.27.	- O.31.d.95.78.
D/152		U.1.b.62.18.	
		U.1.b.92.62.	
		U.1.b.95.75.	
		O.32.c.55.32.	
		O.32.c.59.48.	
		O.32.c.51.61.	

(c) S.O.S.

Appendix 'A' continued   Page ...

(c) **S.O.S. CHERISY SOUTH** -
    This concentration will be ordered in the event of hostile attack limited to the Southern portion of the Left Battalion Front.

    A/152   O.32.c.05.35. - O.32.a.15.33.
    B/152   O.32.a.15.33. - O.32.a.13.85.
    C/152   O.32.a.13.85. - O.26.c.30.33.
    D/152   O.32.c.52.90.
                     O.32.a.48.22.
                     O.32.a.32.64.
                     O.32.a.37.84.
                     O.26.c.50.05.
                     O.26.c.31.32.

(d) **S.O.S. CHERISY NORTH** -
    This concentration will be ordered in the event of hostile attack limited to the Northern portion of the Left Battalion front.

    A/152   O.26.c.22.05. - O.26.c.33.53.
    C/152   O.26.c.33.54. - O.26.c.42.78.
             O.26.c.42.78. - O.26.a.57.00.
    B/152   O.26.a.57.00. - O.26.a.78.48.
    D/152   O.26.c.50.05.
                     O.26.c.51.32.
                     O.26.c.78.68.
                     O.26.b.20.00.
                     O.26.b.08.28.
                     O.26.b.57.55.

(e) Mutual Support -
    (i)   In the event of the Centre Section being attacked but no attack developing on the front of the Right Section, Right Group, R.F.A. will fire as follows on receipt of a message from Centre Group, R.F.A. "Assist Centre Group".

        4   18 pdrs.   Barrage U.1.b.62.18. - 35.62.
        2   4.5" Hows. points U.1.b.62.18, U.1.d.78.90.

    (ii) In the event of the Centre Section being attacked but no attack developing on the front of the Left Section, the Left Group, R.F.A. will fire as follows on receipt of a message from Centre Group, R.F.A. "Assist SAGE".

        8   18 pdrs.   O.26.c.50.75. - O.26.a.80.48.
        6   4.5" Hows. Trench junction in NIGHT LANE

(f) Counter preparation Schemes -
    (i)   Counter Preparation 'A' - This will be fired when the enemy opens an intense fire on our front line system which it is thought will be followed immediately by a hostile attack.

            All Batteries   Normal S.O.S. Lines
        Rate of fire -
            18 pdrs.   4 rounds per gun per min. for first 5 minutes.
                       2 rounds per gun per min. for second 5 "
            4.5" Hows. 2 rounds per gun per min. for first 5 minutes.
                       1 round per gun per min. for second 5 minutes
        followed by steady bombardment.

                                                        (ii) Counter

Counter Preparation Schemes (continued)

(ii) Counter Preparation 'B" - This will be fired in the event of a heavy hostile bombardment of our trenches which it is thought may be followed by a hostile attack after a few hours.

    A/152   1 gun search SENSEE TRENCH.
            1 gun search road in FONTAINE WOOD.
            4 guns sweep front and support lines in own zone between S.O.S. Barrages, also communication trenches leading to front line.

    B & C/
      152   4 guns Sweep front and support lines in own zone, between S.O.S. Barrages.
            2 guns Communication trenches leading to front line.

    D/152 1 How. U.2.a.10.80.
           1 How. O.32.c.90.50.
           1 How. O.32.b.10.05.
           1 How. O.26.c.78.05.
           1 How. O.26.d.84.63.
           1 How. O.28.d.32.92.

Rates of fire -
    Steady bombardment, half S.O.S. rates for first 15 minutes, and continued at rates according to the situation.

(iii) Counter Preparation 'C'- This will be fired in the event of a steady bombardment of our trenches likely to be followed by a hostile attack after some days.
    It will consist of harassing fire on T.M's and O.P's by day and intense harassing fire on communications by night.

APPENDIX "B"

SIGNAL COMMUNICATION -

1..	A tracing (Map 'C') is attached showing the signal communication in the Centre Section.

2..	Speaking telephones will not be used in front of Brigade Headquarters except in cases of emergency.

D3 telephones will not be permanently connected in advance of Brigade Headquarters but will be kept in the charge of an officer at the various Headquarters.

It is the duty of these officers to connect up these telephones immediately in case of alarm.

3..	All means of communication provided will be tested at frequent intervals and messages sent by every means daily.

4..	O.C's Battalions in Support and Brigade Reserve will ensure that the visual signalling stations that have been fixed for the battle positions of each of their respective Companies are known to all concerned and arrangements made for manning them immediately their Companies are ordered to occupy their battle positions.

APPENDIX "C".

INSTRUCTIONS REGARDING THE SENDING OF THE S.O.S. MESSAGE –

1.. The S.O.S. light signal is at present a rifle grenade bursting into 2 RED and 2 GREEN stars.

2.. This signal will be fired from the front line immediately the enemy is seen to be advancing to the attack.

In addition to the above the Commander of a front line post is justified in sending up the S.O.S. in the event of his trench being so heavily bombarded by the enemy as to render it impossible for sentries to keep an adequate look out.

3.. Should the S.O.S. light signal be sent up from the front line, it will also be sent up at once from the Company Headquarters and Battalion Headquarters on whose front it was originally fired and will be repeated until it is obvious that the covering artillery has responded.

4.. A look out man provided with sticks indicating the extent of the front held by the unit concerned will always be on duty at the Headquarters of each Battalion in the line and at the Headquarters of each Company in the front line.

5.. Supplies of S.O.S. rifle grenades will be maintained ready for instant use at every Officer's shelter in the front line, at the H.Q. of every Company in the front line and at the H.Q. of each Battalion in the line.

The Officer on duty in the front line will at all times have a S.O.S. rifle grenade with him ready to be fired at a moment's notice.

Care must be taken to protect these S.O.S. rifle grenades from damp.

6.. Troops on the flanks of a locality from which the S.O.S. light signal has been sent up, will never repeat the signal unless their own front is also threatened at the time.

They will however, forward an immediate report to their Battalion H.Q. for transmission to Brigade H.Q. stating the situation on their front

7.. Whenever the S.O.S. message is sent by light signal it will be confirmed by wire with the least possible delay. The telegram must state the portion of the front threatened: it will then be forwarded automatically by the Signal service to Centre Group, R.F.A. and repeated to all Signal Offices in the Brigade area.

All signal traffic in hand when a S.O.S. telegram is handed in will be stopped at once until the S.O.S. telegram has been sent through.

28031 W3125/M2250 1000m 6/17 M.R.Co.,Ltd. (1367) Forms W3091.   Army Form W. 3091.

Cover for Documents.

Natures of Enclosures.

OPERATION

ORDERS

102ND INF. BDE.

Notes, or Letters written.

SECRET.   Copy No.. 37

102nd INFANTRY BRIGADE ORDER No.. 181
******

Ref. Maps
HENINEL and
GUEMAPPE
Sheets   31 : 12 : 1917.
1:10,000.
---------   --------------------

1.. Reliefs will be carried out as under on JANUARY 2nd 1918 -

  (a) 21st N.F. will relieve 23rd N.F. in Right Subsector.
      Relief to be complete by 11.0 a.m. On relief 23rd N.F.
      will take over positions vacated by 21st N.F. and become
      Battalion in Support.

  (b) 20th N.F. will relieve 22nd N.F. in Left Subsector. 20th N.F.
      not to move before 11.0 a.m. On relief 22nd N.F. will take
      over positions vacated by 20th N.F. and become battalion in
      Brigade Reserve.

2.. All moves will be by parties not greater than platoons at not less
    than 100^x distance.

3.. All aeroplane photographs, reserve S.A.A., grenades, tools, petrol
    tins, other trench stores and all details of work in hand and
    proposed will be handed over between units on relief.
    Lists of stores handed over will be forwarded to Brigade Head-
    quarters by 12 noon January 3rd.

4.. All other details of relief will be arranged direct between C.O's
    concerned.

5.. Completion of relief will be reported to Brigade Headquarters by
    telegraphing the word "DUCK".

    Acknowledge.
                                                        Major.
                                               BRIGADE MAJOR.
                                      102nd (TYNESIDE SCOTTISH) BDE.

Issued at 7.0 p.m. to -

            Brigade Commander ..   Copy No. 1
            Brigade Major   .....   "   "   2
            Staff Captain   ......   "   "   3
            Signals   .... "   "   4
            Bde. Transport Off...   "   "   5
            20th N.F.   .... "   "   6
            21st "   .... "   "   7
            22nd "   .... "   "   8
            23rd "   .... "   "   9
            102 M.G. Coy   .... "   " 10
            102 L.T.M. Bty   .... "   " 11
            34th Division   .... "   " 12
            101st Inf Bde   .... "   " 13
            103rd Inf Bde   .... "   " 14
            Right Group R.F.A...   "   " 15
            208th Field Co R.E...   "   " 16

            Diary and File   .... 17 ---- 18.

SECRET.   Copy No... 17

102nd INFANTRY BRIGADE ORDER No.182.

Ref. Maps.
HENINEL &   5 : 1 : 1918.
GUEMAPPE
1:10,000.

1.. Reliefs will be carried out as under on JANUARY 6TH 1918.-

   (a) 22nd Bn. N.F. will relieve 20th Bn. N.F. in Left
       Subsector. Relief to be complete by 11.0.a.m.

   (b) 20th Bn. N.F. on relief by 22nd Bn.N.F. will relieve
       23rd N.F. and become Battalion in Support.

   (c) 23rd Bn.N.F. on relief by 20th Bn.N.F. will relieve
       21st Bn. N.F. in Right Subsector. 21st Bn. N.F. on
       relief will take over positions in SHAFT AVENUE vacated
       by 22nd Bn. N.F. and become Battalion in Bde. Reserve.

2.. All moves will be by parties not greater than platoons at not
    less than 100 yards distance.

3.. All aeroplane photographs, reserve S.A.A., grenades, tools, petrol
    tins, other trench stores and all details of work in hand and
    proposed will be handed over between Units on relief.
        Lists of stores handed over will be forwarded to Brigade Head-
    quarters by 12 noon, January 7th.

4.. All other details of relief will be arranged direct between C.O's
    concerned.

5.. Completion of relief will be reported to Brigade Headquarters by
    telegraphing the word "MEN".

    ACKNOWLEDGE.
                                                        Major,
                                                      BRIGADE MAJOR,
    Issued at 7.0.a.m. to -   102ND (TYNESIDE SCOTTISH) BDE.

                    Brigade Commander   .. Copy No.1
                    Brigade Major ....   "   " 2
                    Staff Captain ....   "   " 3.
                    Signals ....   "   " 4.
                    Bde. Transport Off...   "   " 5.
                    20th N.F ....   "   " 6.
                    21st N.F ....   "   " 7.
                    22nd N.F ....   "   " 8.
                    23rd N.F ....   "   " 9.
                    102nd L.G.C..........   "   " 10.
                    102nd L.T.M..........   "   " 11.
                    34th Division........   "   " 12.
                    101st Inf. Bde.......   "   " 13.
                    103rd Inf. Bde.......   "   " 14.
                    Centre Group R.F.A..   "   " 15.
                    208th Field Co. R.E   "   " 23.

                    Diary and File   17 - 18.

SECRET.

Appendix I(c)

Copy No. 17

102nd INFANTRY BRIGADE ORDER No. 185.

Ref. Maps
HENINEL &
GUEMAPPE
1:10,000.

9 : 1 : 1918.

1.. Reliefs will be carried out as underon JANUARY 10th, 1918 :-

   (a) - 20th N.F. will relieve 22nd N.F. in Left Subsector. Relief to be complete by 11.0 a.m. On relief 22nd N.F. will take over the positions vacated by 20th N.F. and become Battalion in Support.

   (b) - 21st N.F. will relieve 23rd N.F. in Right Subsector. 21st N.F. not to move before 11.0 a.m. On relief 23rd N.F. will take over positions vacated by 21st N.F. and become Battalion in Brigade Reserve.

2.. All moves will be by parties not greater than platoons at not less than 100 yards distance.

3.. All aeroplane photographs, reserve S.A.A., grenades, tools, petrol tins, other trench stores and all details of work in hand and proposed will be handed over between units on relief.
   Lists of stores handed over will be forwarded to Brigade Headquarters by 12 noon January 11th.

4.. All other details of relief will be arranged direct between C.O's concerned.

5.. Completion of relief will be reported to Brigade Headquarters by telegraphing the word "GROUSE".

ACKNOWLEDGE.

Major.
BRIGADE MAJOR.

Issued at 7.0 a.m. to -   102nd (TYNESIDE SCOTTISH) BDE.

Brigade Commander ...	Copy No. 1
Brigade Major	" " 2
Staff Captain	" " 3
Signals	" " 4
Bde. Transport Off ...	" " 5
20th N.F.	" " 6
21st "	" " 7
22nd "	" " 8
23rd "	" " 9
102nd M.G. Coy	" " 10
102nd L.T.M.B.	" " 11
34th Division	" " 12
101st Inf. Bde	" " 13
103rd Inf. Bde	" " 14
Centre Group R.F.A. ..	" " 15
208th Field Co. R.E...	" " 16
Diary and File	17 - 18.

SECRET. War Diary   Copy No.. 17

102nd INFANTRY BRIGADE ORDER No.. 184

Ref. Maps
HENINEL &
GUEMAPPE.   13th JANUARY, 1918.
1:10,000.

1.. Reliefs will be carried out as under on JANUARY 14th, 1918 —

    (a) 23rd N.F. will relieve 21st N.F. in Right Subsector.
        23rd N.F. not to move before 8.30 a.m. and relief to
        be complete by 12 noon.

    (b) 21st N.F. on relief by 23rd N.F. will relieve 22nd N.F.
        and become Battalion in Support.

    (c) 22nd N.F., on relief by 21st N.F., will relieve 20th N.F.
        in Left Subsector. 20th N.F. on relief will take over
        the accommodation vacated by 23rd N.F. and become Battalion
        in Brigade Reserve.

2.. All moves will be by parties not greater than platoons at not less than 100 yards distance.

3.. All aeroplane photographs, reserve S.A.A., grenades, tools, petrol tins and other trench stores and all details of work in hand and proposed will be handed over between units on relief.
Lists of stores handed over will be forwarded to Brigade Head= quarters by 12 noon January 15th, 1918.

4.. All other details of relief will be arranged direct between C.O's concerned.

5.. Completion of relief will be reported to Brigade Headquarters by telegraphing the word "PHEASANT".

ACKNOWLEDGE.

                                          Major
                              BRIGADE MAJOR
                    102nd (TYNESIDE SCOTTISH) BRIGADE.

Issued at 7.0 a.m. to —

	Copy No.
Brigade Commander	1
Brigade Major	2
Staff Captain	3
Signals	4
Bde. Transport Officer	5
20th N.F.	6
21st "	7
22nd "	8
23rd "	9
102nd M.G. Coy	10
102nd L.T.M.B.	11
34th Division	12
101st Inf. Bde	13
103rd Inf. Bde	14
Centre Group R.F.A.	15
208th Field Co. R.E.	16
Diary and File	17 – 18

SECRET   Copy No ..17

                                                   Appendix I (e)

Ref Map   102nd INFANTRY BRIGADE ORDER No. 185
HENINEL &   **
GUEMAPPE
1:10-000

                                                   16th January- 1918

1.. Reliefs will be carried out as under on January 17th, 1918 -

    (a) 21st N.F. will relieve 23rd N.F. in Right Subsector.
         23rd N.F. on relief will take over the positions vacated
         by 21st N.F. and become Battalion in Support.

    (b) 20th N.F. will relieve 22nd N.F. in Left Subsector.
         On relief 22nd N.F. will take over positions vacated by
         20th N.F. and become Battalion in Brigade Reserve.

2.. The relief of both Forward Battalions will commence directly
    after evening stand down.

3.. Troops must be prepared to move over the open to avoid places
    in the trenches where the mud is deep. Routes for this
    purpose will be reconnoitred previously so as to avoid
    unnecessary damage to the wire.

4.. All aeroplane photographs, reserve S.A.A. grenades, tools,
    petrol tins, other trench stores and all details of work in hand
    and proposed will be handed over between Units on relief.
    Lists of stores handed over will be forwarded to Brigade Head-
    quarters by 6 p.m. January 18th.

5.. All other details of relief will be arranged direct between
    C.O's concerned.

6.. Completion of relief will be reported to Brigade Headquarters
    by telegraphing the word "PARTRIDGE".

    ACKNOWLEDGE.

                                                   Major.
                                            BRIGADE MAJOR.
                                   102nd (TYNESIDE SCOTTISH) BRIGADE.

Issued at 5 p.m. to :-

            Brigade Commander .... Copy No. 1
            Brigade Major ....   "   " 2
            Staff Captain ....   "   " 3
            Signals ....   "   " 4
            Bde. Transport Officer .....   "   " 5
            20th N.F. ....   "   " 6
            21st N.F. ....   "   " 7
            22nd N.F. ....   "   " 8
            23rd N.F. ....   "   " 9
            102nd M.G.Coy. ....   "   " 10
            102nd L.T.M.B. ....   "   " 11
            34th Division ....   "   " 12
            101st Infantry Bde. ....   "   " 13
            103rd Infantry Bde. ....   "   " 14
            Centre Group, R.F.A. ....   "   " 15
            208th Field Co. R.E. ....   "   " 16
            --
            Diary and file ....   "   " 17 - 18

SECRET

Copy No .. 16

Appendix 1(f)

Ref. Map
HENINEL &
GUEMAPPE
1:10,000

102nd INFANTRY BRIGADE ORDER NO .. 186.

17 : 1 : 18

1.. The 102nd Machine Gun Company will be relieved by 103rd Machine Gun Company on January 18th, commencing at evening stand down.

2.. Details of the relief will be arranged direct between O's. C. 102 and 103 Machine Gun Companies.

3.. On completion of the relief, 103rd Machine Gun Coy. will come under the orders of O.C. 102nd Infantry Bde. and the 102nd Machine Gun Company will pass into Divisional Reserve.

4.. The 102nd Machine Gun Company is to be accomodated at HENIN CAMP while in Divisional Reserve.

5.. Completion of relief will be reported to Brigade Headquarters by telegraphing the word "SWIPE".

ACKNOWLEDGE.

Major,
BRIGADE MAJOR,
102nd (TYNESIDE SCOTTISH) BRIGADE.

102 B.H.Q.

Issued at 7.p.m. to :-

Brigade Commander................	Copy No. 1
Brigade Major....................	" " 2
Staff Captain....................	" " 3
Signals..........................	" " 4
Bde. Transport Officer...........	" " 5
20th N.F.........................	" " 6
21st N.F.........................	" " 7
22nd N.F.........................	" " 8
23rd N.F.........................	" " 9
102 Machine Gun Company..........	" " 10
102 Light T.M.Bty................	" " 11
34th Division....................	" " 12
101st Inf. Bde...................	" " 13
103rd Inf. Bde...................	" " 14
103rd M.G.Coy....................	" " 15
Diary and File...................	" " 16 and 17.

S E C R E T   Copy No. .. 17.

Appendix I(q)

Ref Map   102nd INFANTRY BRIGADE ORDER NO.. 187
HENINEL ********************************
& GUEMAPPE
1:10,000

20-1-18

1..   Reliefs will be carried out as under on January 20th, 1918 -

  (a) 23rd N.F. will relieve 21st N.F. in Right Sub-sector. On relief 21st N.F. will take over the positions vacated by 22nd N.F. and become Battalion in Brigade Reserve.

  (b) 22nd N.F. will relieve 20th N.F. in Left Subsector On relief 20th N.F. will take over the positions vacated by 23rd N.F. and become Battalion in Support.

2..   The relief of both battalions in the line will commence directly after evening stand down.

3..   Troops must be prepared to move over the open to avoid places in the trenches where the mud is deep. Routes for this purpose will be reconnoitred previously so as to avoid unnecessary damage to the wire.

4..   All aeroplane photographs, reserve S.A.A., grenades, tools, petrol tins, other trench stores and all details of work in hand and proposed will be handed over between units on relief. Lists of stores handed over will be forwarded to Brigade Headquarters by 6 p.m. January 21st.

5..   All other details of relief will be arranged direct between C.O's concerned.

6..   Completion of relief will be reported to Brigade Headquarters by telegraphing the word "CURLEW"

ACKNOWLEDGE

            Major.
          BRIGADE MAJOR
       102nd (TYNESIDE SCOTTISH) BDE.

Issued at 7 a.m. to -

    Brigade Commander .... Copy No. 1
    Brigade Major .... Copy No. 2
    Staff Captain .... Copy No. 3
    Signals .... Copy No. 4
    Brigade Transport Officer .. Copy No. 5
    20th N.F. .... Copy No. 6
    21st N.F. .... Copy No. 7
    22nd N.F. .... Copy No. 8
    23rd N.F. .... Copy No. 9
    103 Machine Gun Coy. .... Copy No. 10
    102 L.T.M.B. .... Copy No. 11
    34th Division .... Copy No. 12
    101st Inf. Bde. .... Copy No. 13
    103rd Inf. Bde. .... Copy No. 14
    Centre Group R.F.A. .... Copy No. 15
    208th Fld Co. R.E. .... Copy No. 16

    Diary & file .... 17 & 18

SECRET   Copy No... 17

Appendix 1(b)

102nd INFANTRY BRIGADE ORDER NO. 188

Ref Map
HENINEL &
GUEMAPPE
1:10,000

22-1-18

1.. Reliefs will be carried out as under on January 23rd, 1918 -

    (a) 20th N.F. will relieve 22nd N.F. in Left Subsector.
        Relief to commence after 12 noon and be complete by
        4 p.m.
        On relief 22nd N.F. will take over the positions vacated
        by 20th N.F. and become Battalion in Support.

    (b) 21st N.F. will relieve 23rd N.F. in Right Subsector.
        Relief to commence directly after evening stand down.
        On relief 23rd N.F. will take over the positions vacated
        by 21st N.F. and become Battalion in Brigade Reserve.

2.. All moves will be by parties not greater than Platoons at not less than 200^x distance.

3.. All aeroplane photographs, reserve S.A.A., grenades, tools, petrol tins, other trench stores and all details of work in hand and proposed will be handed over between Units on relief.
    Lists of stores handed over will be forwarded to Brigade Headquarters by 6 p.m. January 24th.

4.. All other details of relief will be arranged direct between C.O's concerned.

5.. Completion of relief will be reported to Brigade Headquarters by telegraphing the word BUZZARD.

ACKNOWLEDGE.
                                                                       Major.
                                                            BRIGADE MAJOR.
                              102nd (TYNESIDE SCOTTISH) BRIGADE.

Issued at 7 p.m. to -

                G.O.C. .... Copy No. 1
                Brigade Major .... " 2
                Staff Captain .... " 3
                Signals .... " 4
                Bde. Transport Officer ..... " 5
                20th N.F. .... " 6
                21st N.F. .... " 7
                22nd N.F. .... " 8
                23rd N.F. .... " 9
                103rd Machine Gun Coy ..... " 10
                102 L.T.M.B. .... " 11
                34th Division .... " 12
                101 Inf. Bde. .... " 13
                103 Inf. Bde. .... " 14
                Centre Group, R.F.A. .... " 15
                208 Field Coy. R.E. .... " 16

                Diary and File .... 17 & 18

T.S.48/105.

To:- O.C., 102 L.T.M.Bty.

    O.C., 20th Bn. N.F.   )
          21st "   )   For
          22nd "   )information
          23rd "   )
    Bde. Transport Officer.)
    Headquarters, 34th Division.)

Reference Table 'A' attached this Brigade Order No.189, 102nd L.T.M.Bty. will now be accommodated in YORK LINES, and not in DURHAM LINES. Accommodation in YORK LINES will be reserved for 102nd L.T.M.Bty. by O.C., 23rd Bn. N.F.

P. Brough Lt.
               Major,
          BRIGADE MAJOR,
102 B.H.Q.,   102nd (TYNESIDE SCOTTISH) BDE.
26-1-1918.

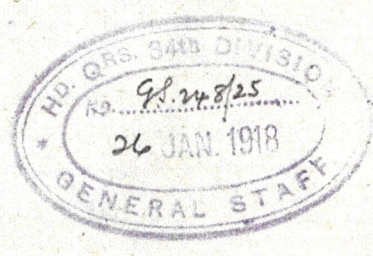

SECRET 　　　　　　　WAR DIARY　　　　　　　Copy No. 21

Ref Maps
HENINEL &
GUEMAPPE
Sheets
1:10,000
51B S.W.
1"20,000.

Appendix 1(j)

102nd INFANTRY BRIGADE ORDER NO. 189

23-1-1918

1.. 34th Division (less artillery) is being relieved in the line by 3rd Division (less artillery) between 25th and 29th January 1918.

On relief 34th Division (less artillery) is to move to the GOMIECOURT area and be in Corps Reserve.

2.. The 102nd Infantry Brigade will be relieved in the Centre Section, 34th Division front by 9th Infantry Brigade in accordance with the attached Table "A".

3.. Orders for the relief of 103rd Machine Gun Company and for the move of 102nd Machine Gun Company are being issued direct by 34th D.M.G.O. to these Machine Gun Companies.

4.. Battalions in the line will leave 1 Officer and 1 N.C.O. per Company with relieving Battalion for 24 hours after completion of relief.

5.. All moves East of ST. MARTIN SUR COJEUL will be by parties not greater than platoons at distances of not less than 200Y.

6.. Units will each send advance parties not exceeding 1 Officer and 5 O.R. to take over billets in the MERCATEL area at 2 p.m. on the day on which they move into this area.

7.. Defence and Pursuit Schemes, all information about the enemy, a statement of work in hand and proposed, aeroplane photographs, trench maps, reserve S.A.A. and grenades, S.O.S. signal lights, L.T.M. bombs, and all other trench stores will be handed over to relieving Units during daylight on the day of relief.

Receipted lists of stores handed over will be forwarded to Brigade Headquarters not later than 12 hours after completion of relief

8.. All other details of relief will be arranged direct between C.O's concerned

9.. 1st Battn. Northd. Fus. and 4th Battn. Royal Fusiliers will come under the orders of G.O.C. 102nd Infantry Brigade from the time at which they arrive at the rendezvous for guides on January 25th until the O.C. 9th Infantry Brigade assumes command of the Centre Section at 11 a.m. January 27th.

10.. Completion of relief will be reported to Brigade Headquarters by telegraphing the word 'HERON'.

11.. Command ..

(2)

11..   Command of the Centre Section, 34th Division front will pass to O.C. 9th Infantry Brigade at 11 a.m. January 27th

12..   102nd Infantry Brigade Headquarters will close at M.22.d.4.4. at 6 p.m. January 27th and re-open at M.35.c.8.0. at the same hour.

ACKNOWLEDGE.

[signature]

Major.
BRIGADE MAJOR.
102nd (TYNESIDE SCOTTISH) BRIGADE.

Issued at 7 p.m. to -

G.O.C.	Copy No.	1
Brigade Major	*	2
Staff Captain	*	3
Signals	*	4
Bde. Transport Officer	*	5
20th N.F.	*	6
21st N.F.	*	7
22nd N.F.	*	8
23rd N.F.	*	9
102nd M.G. Coy.	*	10
103rd M.G. Coy.	*	11
102 L.T.M.B.	*	12
34th Division	*	13
101st Infantry Bde.	*	14
103rd Infantry Bde.	*	15
9th Infantry Bde.	*	16
1st Bn. Northd. Fus.	*	17
4th Bn. Royal Fusiliers	*	18
Centre Group, R.F.A.	*	19
208th Field Coy. R.E.	*	20
Diary and file		21 & 22

Table 'A'.   To accompany 2nd Inf. Bde. Order No. 189

DATE	Unit	Relieved In	Guides Number	Guides Place	Time	ROUTES In	ROUTES Out	Destinatn of outgoing Unit	Takes over billets from	REMARKS
Jan. 25th	22nd N.F.	Support	1 per Platoon, 1 for Bn. HQ	H.23.c.9.3.	5 pm	1 Co.SHAFT TR.remainder FOSTER AV.	FOSTER & FIRST AVENUES	Northd. Lines.	1st A.F.	
Jan. 25th	23rd N.F.	4th R.F. Reserve	1 per Coy. 1 for Bn.HQ	H.23.c.9.3.	6 pm	SHAFT TR.	SHAFT TR.	York Lines	4th R.F.	
Jan. 25th	20th N.F.	1st N.F. Left Sub-Sector	To be arranged between C.O's concerned					Support position		Relief to commence after 12 noon & be complete by 4 pm
Jan. 25th	21st N.F.	4th R.F. Right Sub-sector	To be arranged by C.O's concerned.					Bde. Reserve		Relief to commence directly after evening stand down
Jan. 27th	20th N.F.	13th King's Support	1 per platoon, 1 for Bn.HQ	H.23.d.4.0.	5 pm	1 Co.SHAFT TR.remainder FOSTER AV.	FOSTER & FIRST AVENUES	DURHAM LINES 'A'	13th King's	
Jan. 27th	21st N.F.	12th W. YORKS Reserve	1 per Coy. 1 for Bn. H.Q.	H.23.d.4.0.	6 pm	SHAFT TR.	SHAFT TR.	DURHAM LINES 'B'	12th W. Yorks	
Jan. 27th	102 MGC	9th LTMB Centre Section	To be arranged by O.C's Batteries concerned.					DURHAM LINES	9th LTMB	

Army Form W. 3091.

Cover for Documents.

Natures of Enclosures.

Appendix 2

Daily Intelligence Summaries

102ND INF. BDE.

Notes, or Letters written.

WAR DIARY
INTELLIGENCE SUMMARY

HQ 102 Infantry Brigade

January 1918

Place	Date	Hour	Summary of Events and Information	Remarks and references to Appendices
N.22.d.4.4. Sheet 51B. SW	1	–	O.O. 181 issued Dec 31st 1917. attached	appendix 1(a)
"	2nd	–	Relief carried out in accordance with O.O. 181.	
"	5th	–	O.O. 182 issued	appendix 1(b)
"	6th	–	Relief carried out in accordance with O.O. 182.	
"	9th	–	O.O. 183 issued	appendix 1(c)
"	10th	–	Relief carried out in accordance with O.O. 183. Three enemy	
"	11th	–	Three Prisoners captured	
"	13th	–	O.O. 184 issued	appendix 1(d)
"	14th	–	Relief carried out in accordance with O.O. 184.	
"	15th	–	Rapid fire carried much damage to trenches	
"	16th	–	O.O. 185 issued	appendix 1(e)
"	17th	–	Relief carried out in accordance with O.O. 185. O.O. 186 issued	appendix 1(f)
"	18th	–	Relief of 102nd MGC by 103rd M.G.Co. carried out in accordance with O.O. 186.	

Army Form C. 2118.

WAR DIARY
or
INTELLIGENCE SUMMARY.

(Erase heading not required.)

January 1918. H.Q. 102 Inf. Bde.

Instructions regarding War Diaries and Intelligence Summaries are contained in F.S. Regs., Part II. and the Staff Manual respectively. Title pages will be prepared in manuscript.

Place	Date	Hour	Summary of Events and Information	Remarks and references to Appendices
M22.d.4.4 Sheet 51 B.S.W	20th	—	O.O. 187 issued. Relief carried out in accordance with O.O. 187.	Appendix 1 (a)
"	21st	—	Brigadier General N.A. Thomson D.S.O. returned from leave and resumed command 102nd Inf. Bde.	Appendix 1 (b)
"	22nd	—	O.O. 188 issued	Appendix 1 (c)
"	23rd	—	Relief carried out in accordance with O.O. 188. O.O. 189 issued	
"	24th	—	Relief carried out in accordance with O.O. 189.	
"	26th	—	Relief carried out in accordance with O.O. 189. 102 M.G.s. was attached 52nd Division	
"	27th	—	Relief carried out in accordance with O.O. 189. Bde Hqs in front York lines instead of in Graham lines.	
M3.b.c.8.0	28th	—	2/2 & 2/2 M.G. commenced Firing.	
	30th	—	2/4 & 2/3 M.G. commenced Firing. Bde Hqs moved to M36.c.8.0 at 6p. 102 Lt TMB	
			Daily Intelligence summaries attached. Dispositions reports attached Casualties during January 1918 Honours & Awards January 1918 Defence scheme	Appendix 2 Appendix 3 Appendix 4 Appendix 5 Appendix 6

Wm Thomson
Brigadier General
comdg 102 Inf Bde.

Appendix 4

CASUALTIES

January 1918.

OFFICERS.

NIL.

OTHER RANKS.

	Killed.	Wounded.	Missing.
20th. Bn. Northd. Fus.)	1	4	-
21st. " "	4	5	1
22nd. " "	1	4	-
23rd. " "	1	6	-
102nd. L.T.M.Btty.	-	2	-
	7	21	1

List of Honours and Awards - January 1918.

Appendix 5

Staff.

D.S.O.
Major F.G.Trobridge, Brigade Major, 102nd Infantry Bde.

※=※=※=※=※=※=※=※=※=※=※=※

20th Bn. North'd. Fus.

D.S.O.
Lt. Col. W.A.Farquhar.

M.C.
Captain B.P.Whillis.

Mentioned in Despatches.
Captain A.P.Ker.
A/Captain J.Thomson.

30200 Pte. F.W.Beaumont.

※=※=※=※=※=※=※=※=※=※=※=※

21st Bn. North'd. Fus.

D.C.M.
21/345 Pte. W.Simpson.

Mentioned in Despatches.
Lt. Col. E.P.Lloyd.
2/Lieut. G.H.Graham.

21/763 Pte. W.Hedley.

※=※=※=※=※=※=※=※=※=※=※=※

22nd Bn. North'd. Fus.

D.C.M.
38233 Cpl. H.F.Welfare.

Mentioned in Despatches.
Lt. Col. Spencer Acklom. D.S.O. M.C.
Captain C.E.Hardy.
Captain A.W.D.Mark, D.S.O., M.C.

22/1102 Sgt. R.E.Johnson.

※=※=※=※=※=※=※=※=※=※=※=※

23rd Bn. North'd. Fus.

M.C.
2/Lieut. D.Scott.

D.C.M.
25/943 L/Cpl. A.Devenish.

Mentioned in Despatches.
Lt. Col. G.Charlton.
Lt. Col. C.P.Porch, D.S.O.
Captain A.Wilson, R.A.M.C. -(M.O.attached).
Lieut. G.Metcalfe.
40781 L/Cpl. F.Smith.

※=※=※=※=※=※=※=※=※=※=※=※

102nd Machine Gun Coy.

D.C.M.
12904 Sgt. Hutchins.

Mentioned in Despatches.
Lieut. G.K.Steinberg.

※=※=※=※=※=※=※=※=※=※=※=※

102nd L.T.M.B.

M.C.
Captain C.N.Levin.

※=※=※=※=※=※=※=※=※=※=※=※

Belgian CROIX DE GUERRE.
48040 L/Cpl. D.Cameron, 20th Bn. North'd. Fus.
22/216. Sgt. J.McCourt, 22nd Bn. North'd. Fus.
10,000. Pte.(L/Cpl) J.W.Ronald, 102nd Machine Gun Coy.

※=※=※=※=※=※=※=※=※=※=※=※

INTELLIGENCE SUMMARY
102nd (TYNESIDE SCOTTISH) BRIGADE.
From 9.0 a.m. 31:12:17 -- 9.0 a.m. 1:1:1918.

A - OUR ACTIVITY -

1.. Artillery -
   Normal activity. Enemy trenches FONTAINE WOOD, CHERISY, and back areas were periodically shelled.

2.. T.M's -
   Our L.T.M's carried out the following shoots -

Rds.	Target.
25	U. 2. a. 26. 35.
10	O. 32. c. 26. 60.
15	O. 32. c. 20. 26.
21	O. 32. s. 40. 58.
30	O. 26. c. 50. 05.
15	O. 26. c. 78. 68.
10	O. 26. a. 60. 03.

   Total fired.. 126 Rds.

3.. M.G's - NIL.

4.. Aircraft -
   2 of our machines crossed enemy lines during the morning.

B - ENEMY ACTIVITY -

1.. Artillery -
   Hostile artillery was active throughout the day. The following trenches were shelled -

   BULLFINCH SUPPORT - 2 direct hits.
   CURTAIN SUPPORT
   PIONEER ALLEY
   CUCKOO TRENCH
   BROWN SUPPORT
   TANK TRENCH ----- 1 direct hit.

   Back areas were also shelled at frequent intervals especially the vicinity between HENINEL and WANCOURT.

2.. T.M's -
   The following targets were engaged by hostile T.M's -

   L.T.M's - Posts 17 and 19, WOOD TR. and FIRST AVENUE.
   H.T.M's - BULLFINCH SUPPORT, CURTAIN SUPPORT, PIONEER ALLEY

   No damage reported.

3.. M.G's - quiet.

4.. Aircraft - At 9.0 a.m. an enemy aeroplane flew over our lines. It was engaged by A.A. and L.G. fire.

C.. INTELLIGENCE -

1.. Movement -
   (a) 11.15 a.m. 7 men carrying timber about 6ft long were observed walking towards HENDECOURT along the FONTAINE--HENDECOURT Rd.
   (b) 11.20 a.m. 7 men were seen to enter ULSTER TR. from the FONTAINE-HENDECOURT Rd.
   (c) 1.0 p.m... Considerable movement in U.3.b. and d.
   (d) 4 - 4.20 pm 8 limbered wagons were observed moving S.W. on the DURY--HENDECOURT Rd. They halted at U.6.b.80.30 and U.5.d.70.10. 1 wagon proceeded across country to UPTON TR. (U.5.b.) where it was met by a party of 12 men from this trench.

C... INTELLIGENCE - contd.

2.. Signals -

(i) At 7.10 p.m. red lights were sent in enemy's front and rear lines. Hostile artillery opened fire on back areas, otherwise no apparent action.

(ii) Signalling was seen S.E. of CHERISY (O.33.a.) no message picked up.

3.. Miscellaneous -
A wide entrance appears to have been made at the Southern end of SUN QUARRY (O.33.c.) - men were seen to enter at this point.

Major.
BRIGADE MAJOR.
1 : 1 : 1918.   102nd (TYNESIDE SCOTTISH) BDE.

PATROLS

1.. A patrol of 1 N.C.O. and 3 O.R's left No. 15 post (O.31.b.77.88.) at 5.30 p.m. Having proceeded 50 yds. sounds of transport could distinctly be heard on the Sunken Rd. about O.32.a.90.65. Dogs were barking in this locality also. The patrol then went forward to about O.32.a.05.75. then to O.32.a.10.50. From the latter point shouting was heard.
   No hostile parties were seen and the patrol returned to our lines at 7.0 p.m.

2.. A N.C.O. and 3 O.R's left No. 19 Post at 9.20 p.m. and patrolled No Man's Land. Patrol returned at 11.35 p.m. through No.22 post. No enemy were seen or heard.

3.. At 11.30 p.m. a N.C.O's patrol left LONE SAP (O.25.d.) and proceeded in a N. direction for 250 yds. The patrol reports sounds of hammering from enemy line at approximately O.26.c.30.10. Stamping of feet could also be heard. The patrol returned to 17.a. post at 1.0 a.m.

4.. Patrols sent out from Right Battalion fron report No Man's Land clear of the enemy and no unusual movement on his part. Sounds were heard occasionally of the enemy working in his front line trench (FORRARD TR.)

Major
BRIGADE MAJOR.
1: 1 : 1918.   102nd (TYNESIDE SCOTTISH) BDE.

War Diary G58

INTELLIGENCE SUMMARY
102nd (TYNESIDE SCOTTISH) BDE.
From 9.0 a.m. 1:1:1918 --- 9.0 a.m. 2:1:1918.

A - OUR ACTIVITY -

1. **Artillery -**
   Normal activity on CHERISY, CHERRY BRIDGE, FONTAINE WOOD, and enemy trenches.

2. **T.M's -**
   (a) L.T.M.B. -
   The following shoots were carried out by our L.T.M's -

Rds.	Target.	
20	Cross Roads	U.1.d.75.95.
18	Sunken Road	U.1.b.50.45.
24	Fork Roads	O.32.b.1.0.
34	Trench Junct.	O.25.b.87.45.
25	Front Line	O.26.a.60.05.

   Total 117 Rounds.

3. **M.G's -**
   Our Vickers guns fired 250 rounds on anti-aircraft work - Nil otherwise.

4. **Aircraft -**
   Four of our machines were observed over the enemy lines. Bombs were dropped on the enemy front line.
   At 3.50 p.m. one of our aeroplanes descended at approx. U.1.b.50.02. The occupants were captured by the enemy.

B - ENEMY ACTIVITY -

1. **Artillery -**
   Quieter than usual. During the day the following targets were engaged -
   (a) BULLFINCH SUPPORT.
   (b) DODO TRENCH - (shrapnel).
   (c) PELICAN DUMP - (4.2).
   (d) KENNEL - (4.2)

2. **T.M's -**
   FOSTER AVENUE, BULLFINCH SUPPORT, and front line between posts 19 and 20 were engaged by hostile trench mortars, chiefly "pineapples"

3. **M.G's -**
   Quiet - Occasional bursts throughout the night.

4. **Aircraft -**
   Enemy aircraft were over our lines at 9.15 a.m., 10.30 a.m. and 3.0 p.m. In all cases they were actively engaged by A.A., M.G. and Lewis Gun fire.

C - INTELLIGENCE -

1. **Movement -** observation difficult.
   (a) 7.55 a.m. - Four men observed working with shovels at U.32.c.55.60. A M.G. is suspected here owing to the constant individual movement to and fro throughout the day.
   (b) - Usual movement around CHERISY and SUN QUARRY.

2. Signals - NIL.

2:1:1918.

A.H. Davies 2/Lt.
for Major.
BRIGADE MAJOR.
102nd (TYNESIDE SCOTTISH) BDE.

To accompany Intell. S.51

:- PATROLS :-

1.. An Officers and 3 O.R's left No. 2 post at 5.30 p.m. for the purpose of examining the enemy's wire in U.1.b. The patrol moved Eastwards then S.E. on striking the Sunken Road. The wire was found to be thick and composed chiefly of Knife rests. Nothing was heard or seen of the enemy and the patrol returned to our lines.

2.. At 8.50 p.m. a Serjeant and 4 O.R's left No. 10 post to reconnoitre enemy sap at O.32.c.2.8. The following information was obtained -

    (i) - the sape is held - coughing heard.
    (ii) - the sap is wired on flanks.
    (iii) - the main belt of wire was unbroken.
    (iv) - no advanced shell holes showed signs of recent occupation.

No hostile parties were encountered and the patrol returned to our lines 9.50 p.m.

3.. A patrol of 1 N.C.O. and 4 O.R's left No. 19 post at 8.0 p.m. Sounds of men working could be heard about O.28.a.60.00. No enemy were seen however.

4.. At 1.0 a.m. a patrol of 1 N.C.O. and 4 O.R's left LONE SAP and proceeded parallel with the Sunken Road, a post is suspected at O.26.c.34.86. The enemy wire was examined and found to be in good condition - no gaps were visible. The patrol continued in N. direction and on reaching the Sunken Road O.26.a.30.74 they were challenged. Rifle fire was opened for a short time and our patrol then entered No. 18 post.

5.. Patrol leaving No. 12 post at 8.0 p.m. reports sounds as if material was being dumped at O.32.a.20.57. Talking and shouting could also be heard. No hostile patrols were encountered and our lines were entered at 9.15 p.m.

                                              Major

2 : 1 : 1918.   BRIGADE MAJOR,
                102nd (TYNESIDE SCOTTISH) BDE.

War Diary

Intell. G. 52

102nd (TYNESIDE SCOTTISH) BDE.
INTELLIGENCE SUMMARY.
From 9.0 a.m. 2:1:1918 - 9.0 a.m. 3:1:1918.

A - OUR ACTIVITY -

1. ARTILLERY -
Our 18-pdrs. fired on enemy trenches and at 6.30 p.m. several salvoes were fired into FONTAINE-lez-CROISILLES.
At 6.30 p.m. and 9.30 p.m. 6" Hows. fired several rounds on the enemy ~~front and support~~ trenches.

2. T.M's -
(a) The following targets were engaged by our Light T.M's -

Target.	Rounds.
U.1.b.75.75	15
U.1.b.90.80	15
O.32.a.45.30	15
O.32.a.55.45	15
O.26.c.62.05	9
O.26.d.00.90	10
Total ..	79 rounds.

(b) H.T.M's -
Between 3.0 p.m. and 4.0 p.m. several H.T.M's (9.45) were fired into CHERISY.

3. M.G's -
Our Vickers guns fired on the following targets -

Time.	Rounds.	Target.
11.15 p.m. to 11.30 p.m	500	O.26.d.78.71.
8.15 p.m. to 8.30 p.m	1000	S.O.S. Line.
10.45 a.m.	650	Aircraft.

4. Aircraft -
Our aeroplanes were active over enemy lines between 10.0 a.m. and 12.30 p.m. At 12.30 p.m. and 4.0 p.m. 2 bombs were dropped on enemy's support trench approximately O.32.c.42.20.

B - ENEMY ACTIVITY -

1. ARTILLERY -
Hostile artillery activity normal.

12.30 p.m.	25 rds.	77 m.m.	SWIFT SUPPORT.
12.45 p.m.	5 :	5.9's	PIONEER ALLEY (slight damage).
2.0 p.m. &) 4.0 p.m...)	20 :	77 mm & 5.9	CURTAIN SUPPORT.
4.30 p.m.	10 :	4.2	PUFFIN AVENUE (O.31.c.20.80)
8.30 - 10 p.m. ...	occasional shelling.		SUPPORT LINE.
6.0 - 8.0 p.m..	18 :	4.2 ...	CONCRETE TRENCH.
9.30 p.m.	12 :	4.2 ...	FOSTER CUCKOO DUMP - 2 direct hits on CUCKOO TRENCH.

2. T.M's -
Hostile mortars were more active than usual, mainly on posts in front line.
At 8.10 p.m. the enemy heavily bombarded our front and support trenches near PIONEER ALLEY held by the Centre and Left Company of the Right Battalion with both Heavy and Light T.M's.
The bombardment continued till 8.25 p.m. after which hostile T.M's were very quiet.

3. M.G's -
Very active during hostile T.M. bombardment.

4. Aircraft -
At 11.30 a.m. a large hostile aeroplane flew low over our lines.

C - INTELLIGENCE -

1. Movement -
   (a) Individual movement around O.32.c.80.45. At 2.45 p.m. an Officer was seen to leave this spot and move towards enemy front lines.

   (b) Individual movement around FONTAINE WOOD.

   (c) 7.0 a.m. - 8.0 a.m. 3.1.18 - about 10 limbers observed moving S.W. along the DURY-HENDECOURT Rd. They were each followed by a party of 8 or 10 men. The limbers halted at U.5.d.70.10 and small groups of men from direction of UNICORN TRENCH and ULSTER TRENCH walked up to them.

   (d) 7.0 a.m. - 8.0 a.m. 3.1.18 - about 40 men were seen in ULSTER TRENCH.

2. Signals -
   2 Signal lamps were observed due E. of posts 8.A. and 10.A. at about 2,000 yds. range.

                                                    Major.
                                            BRIGADE MAJOR.
3:1:18.   102nd (TYNESIDE SCOTTISH) BDE.

- PATROLS -
                                    To accompany Intell.G.52.

1.. A patrol of 1 N.C.O. and 4 O.R's left No. 14 post at 1.0 a.m. and reports that the wire across the Sunken Rd. about O.32.a.1.9. to be good, consisting of knife rests and concertinas.

2.. Patrol leaving LONE SAP at 11.0 p.m. neither heard or saw any signs of the enemy.

3.. A N.C.O's patrol left No. 19 post at 8.0 p.m. and proceeded due E. On reaching the enemy wire 2 bombs were thrown from about O.26.c.55.95. Patrol waited for 20 minutes, then returned to our lines.

4... A patrol which left No. 2 post at 7.10 p.m. was forced to return at 8.10 p.m. owing to hostile M.G. fire and T.M. bombardment.

                                                    Major.
                                            BRIGADE MAJOR
3:1:18.   102nd (TYNESIDE SCOTTISH) BDE

INTELLIGENCE SUMMARY
102nd (TYNESIDE SCOTTISH) BRIGADE.
From 9 a.m. 3-1-1918 – 9 a.m. 4-1-1918

A. OUR ACTIVITY
1. Artillery –
   Our 18 pdrs. fired on enemy trenches and CHERISY.
   At 12.30 p.m. and 4.30 p.m. hostile trenches in O.32.a. and O.32.c. were shelled by 4.5 hows.
   Back areas were shelled intermittently throughout the 24 hours.

2. Trench Mortars –
   (a) L.T.M.B.
   Our light trench mortars fired on the following targets –

TARGET	ROUNDS
U.1.b.74.75.	15
U.1.b.92.68.	10
O.32.c.53.00.	30
U.1.b.65.15.	30
O32.a.42.60.	15
O.32.a.55.45.	10
O.32.a.55.80.	30
Rds.	140

   (b) 6" Stokes –
   At intervals during the day about 60 rounds were fired at selected targets in the enemy's front and support trenches.

3. Machine Guns –
   Our Vickers guns expended 1400 rounds on the following targets –

TIME	ROUNDS	TARGET
11.5 pm – 11.35 pm)	750	O.27.c.30.90.
7 am – 7.15 am)		
7.15 am	250	O.26.d.78.72.
10.45 am – 11.15 am	400	Aircraft.

4. Aircraft –
   Our aeroplanes were active during the morning. Aircraft flew over the enemy lines at the following times – 8 a.m. 9 a.m. 10.15 a.m., 11.20 a.m., 12 noon, 2 p.m., 3 p.m. – 4.30 p.m. At 8 a.m. a bomb was dropped between the enemy front and support lines.

B. ENEMY ACTIVITY –
1. Artillery –
   The usual activity took place on our trenches and back areas – with all calibres.

2. T.M's –
   Hostile mortars were fairly active.
   7.30 am 3 H.T.M's on No. 14 Post (suspected gun emplacement at O.32.b.5.8.)
   9 – 11 pm 15 H.T.M's in vicinity of SWIFT SUPPORT.
   Many pineapples were fired on our front line.

3. Machine Guns –
   Intermittent fire during the night along our front line.

4. Aircraft –
   Enemy aircraft attempted to cross our lines at 7 a.m. 10 – 10.30 am 11 am – 1 pm and 2.30 p.m.
   At 11 am a hostile plane dropped 2 magnesium flares just West of No. 15 post with no apparent result.

C. INTELLIGENCE
1. Movement –
   (a) 6 – 6.30 am. Much movement in U.4.d. & U.10.a.
   (b) 8 – 9 am Small party working on HENDECOURT-DURY Rd. in U.6.b. A wagon drawn by 2 horses proceeding towards HENDECOURT stopped at this point & was unloaded.

INTELLIGENCE
Movement (continued)

      (c) 12 am - 12.40 pm. Much movement around UPTON WOOD & UPTON QUARRY.
      (d) 12.noon. A motor car travelling at high speed making for CHERISY along the CHERISY - HENDECOURT Rd.
      (e) 3 p.m. Enemy limber unloaded at U.3.b.72.30.
      (f) 3 pm   "   "   "   " U.6.b.70.20.
      (g) 4.10 pm - 4.20 pm. 9 limbers on DURY-HENDECOURT Rd.

      A small mound of new earth can be seen at O.22.a.8.7.

2. Signals -
   (1) Two red lights were fired opposite No. 14 Post at 2 am. No apparent action.

   Miscellaneous -
   (2) A hostile battery is suspected at O.35.d.40.90. (Gun flashes observed).

102 B.H.Q.
4-1-1918.

for Major.
BRIGADE MAJOR
102nd (TYNESIDE SCOTTISH) BRIGADE.

PATROLS

1. A patrol leaving our lines at 9.10 p.m. from No. 4 Post reports enemy wire about U.1.b.60.19. to be knee deep.

2. A patrol left No. 7 Post at 9 p.m. and reports that the enemy wire between O.32.a.2.2. and O.32.c.1.5. to be strong, and no gaps were found. Coughing and talking could be heard in the enemy trench, but no hostile parties were seen in "NO MAN'S LAND".

3. A patrol of 1 Officer and 6 O.R.'s left No. 21 Post & at 8 p.m. They proceeded N to the enemy wire then turned S.W. When about O.26.a.70.20. a M.G. opened fire and 3 rifle grenades were also fired. The patrol took cover and waited for 20 minutes and returned to No. 19 Post at 9.50 p.m.

4. 1 N.C.O. and 4 men left No. 18 Post at 6. a.m. They proceeded along the Sunken road to within 60 yards of the enemy wire when hostile fires was opened on them. The patrol remained in their position for 15 minutes and nothing further happened. No. 18 Post was entered at 7.15 A.m.

5. "DAWN PATROLS" report no unusual activity on the part of the enemy.

A.H.Davies
2/L
for Major.
BRIGADE MAJOR.
102 B.H.Q.
4-1-1918.
102nd (TYNESIDE SCOTTISH) BDE.

Intell. G.

INTELLIGENCE SUMMARY
102nd (TYNESIDE SCOTTISH) BRIGADE.
From 9.0 a.m. 4:1:1918 -- 9.0 a.m. 5:1:1918.

A - OUR ACTIVITY -
1.. Artillery -

Our 18-pdrs fired bursts at intervals on FONTAINE WOOD, CHERISY, and enemy front and support trenches. Between 11.0 a.m. and 1.0 pm back areas were shelled.

2.. T.M's -

(a) L.T.M.'s -

The following shoots were carried out -

Target.	Rounds.
U. 1 .b. 90. 65.	20
U. 1. b. 75. 75.	10
O. 32. a. 40. 80.	20
O. 32. a. 55. 80.	15
Total ..	65 rounds.

(b) 6" Stokes -
Between 3 and 4.0 p.m. 20 rounds were fired on SENSEE TRENCH (U.2.c.).

(c) H.T.M.'s -
10 rounds were fired on CHERISY between 2 and 3.0 p.m.

3.. M.G's -
Between 11.15 p.m. and 12.0 p.m. our Vickers guns fired 1,000 rounds on U. 2. a. 70. 09.

4.. Aircraft -
Much activity during the morning and early afternoon. Our 'planes were observed over enemy lines at the following times -
7.30 a.m., 8.0 a.m. 9.0 a.m., 11.0 a.m., at intervals between 11.0 am and 1.0 p.m. and 2.45 p.m.
At 4.0 p.m. one of our aeroplanes engaged an E.A. and drove it off.

B - ENEMY ACTIVITY -

1.. Artillery -
There was little hostile artillery activity on our trenches. FIRST AVENUE,(2 direct hits at N.36.d.90.60), SWIFT SUPPORT and CURTAIN SUPPORT were the chief targets. The area around HENINEL was shelled at frequent intervals with all calibres.

2.. T.M's -
Quiet. Some granatenwerfers were fired on the front line.

3.. M.G's -
Hostile M.G's were more active than usual between evening stand-to and 11.0 p.m. - traversing fire along our front line parapet.

4.. Aircraft -
E.A. were over our lines at 8.0 a.m., 9.15 a.m. 12.30 p.m. and 4.0 p.m. In all cases they were "turned" by our A.A. fire.

C - INTELLIGENCE -
1.. Movement -
9.10 a.m. much movement to and from SUN QUARRY (O.33.c.)
4.15 p.m. movement was seen for the first time in enemy's front line trench at U.1.b.61.50. The trench here appears to be shallow.

- 2 -

C - INTELLIGENCE - contd.

1. Movement - contd.

   7 - 8 a.m. (5.1.18) 3 wagons moved away from U.4.b.70.55 and went across country towards the DURY-HENDECOURT Rd. (U.6.)

2. Signals .. Nil.

3. Work -

   1. A box loophole has been constructed at Q.33.c.70.20 and more work has been done at the S. end of SUN QUARRY.

   2. During the night parts have been taken away from the derelict aeroplane lying in the enemy's wire in U.1.b.

```
                                                          Major
102 B. H. Q.                          BRIGADE MAJOR
5 : 1 : 18                    102nd (TYNESIDE SCOTTISH) BDE.
```

To accompany Intell G. 53

* PATROLS *

1. A patrol of 1 N.C.O. and 4 men left No. 19 post (O.26.a.21.00) at 8.0 p.m. On passing through our wire rifle fire was opened on them. No signs of the enemy could be seen so that the patrol advanced in an E. direction to the enemy wire, then turned N. for a distance of 100 yds. As the party were returning to our lines they were again fired on, still no signs were seen of the enemy. No. 21 post was entered at 9.15 p.m.

2. A patrol left our lines at O.31.b.78.20 and reports that there are no gaps in enemy wire between O.32.a.2.2 and O.32.c.1.5. The enemy was heard in his trenches.

3. The enemy wire at U.1.b.50.60 is reported to be high and very thick. It consists of knife rests with much loose wire intermingled. No gaps or weak places were discovered. Walking and coughing were also heard. The patrol returned to our lines at 12.35 a.m.

4. An Officers and 4 O.R's left LONE Sap at 11.0 p.m. and proceeded E. to the enemy wire. The wire from here to 100 yds N. of this point is 3 ft. 6 ins. high and from 4 ft. to 6 ft. deep. It consists mainly of concertina and knife rests. No gaps were found.

5. A patrol from No. 14 post reports working being carried on about O.32.a.18.71. Coughing was also heard. The wire was found to be good, and no gaps existed. No. 12 post was entered at 2.40 a.m.

```
                                                          Major
102 B. H. Q.                          BRIGADE MAJOR
5 : 1 : 1918.                 102nd (TYNESIDE SCOTTISH) BDE.
```

War Diary

INTELLIGENCE SUMMARY
102nd (TYNESIDE SCOTTISH) BRIGADE.
FROM 9 a.m. 5-1-18 - 9 a.m. 6-1-18

A. OUR ACTIVITY

1. Artillery -
   Our 18 pdrs. and 4.5 hows were more active than usual. Shoots were carried out on CHERISY, FONTAINE - Les - CROISILLES, enemy trenches and back areas.

2. Trench Mortars -
   (a) L.T.M's. -
   The following targets were engaged with good effect -

TARGET	ROUNDS
U.1.b.20.25.	25
0.32.a.52.20.	15
60.26.c.54.68.	10
0.26.c.55.40.	50
	90

   (b) 2" Newtons -
       11.20 a.m. 10 rounds ARESEE TRENCH (U.2.a.)
       11.50 a.m. 15 rounds 0.32.c.19.52.
       3.15 p.m. 15 rounds FONTAINE WOOD.

   (c) H.T.M's. -
       2 - 3 p.m.   6 rounds   CHERISY.

3. Machine guns -
   Our Vickers guns expended 250 rounds on the following target -

TIME	ROUNDS	TARGET
11.30 pm	250	U.2.a.20.42.

4. Aircraft -
   Our aeroplanes crossed enemy lines at 7.30 a.m., 8 a.m., 1.45 pm, 3 p.m. and 4 p.m.

B. ENEMY ACTIVITY -

1. Artillery -
   Enemy activity was below normal. Slight shelling of our trenches took place at intervals, more especially on the Right Battalion front.
   Back areas were comparatively free from hostile shelling.

2. Trench Mortars -
   Between 1 - 2 p.m. 6 H.T.M's fell on Post line of Left Battalion (This mortar appears to be firing from 0.32.b.1.2.) Other hostile activity was confined to granatenwerfers.

3. Machine guns -
   There was intermittent firing throughout the night. Hostile M.G's were very active on the Right Battalion front between the hours of 11 p.m. and 1 a.m.

4. Aircraft -
   E.A. less active than usual. Hostile planes crossed our lines at 11 am, 1 p.m. and 2.40 p.m.

C. INTELLIGENCE

1. Movement. -
   (a) 8.10 a.m.   Wagon unloaded at U.3.d.70.10.
   ((b) 8.20 a.m.   12 men left FONTAINE WOOD and walked to SUNKEN ROAD
                     U.3.b.60.50.

(c) ...

2

C. INTELLIGENCE
   Movement - (continued) -

   (c) Individual movement around SUN QUARRY.
   (d) 4.10 - 4.55 p.m. 12 limbers moved S.W. along BURY—HENDECOURT
                         Rd. Some stopped on road in U.3.c. and U.3.d.
                         Others moved N. on roads in U.3.b. and d.,
                         U.3.a. and c. and 5 limbers moved along Sunken
                         Road in U.4.c. About 100 men left UNICORN &
                         ULSTER TRENCHES and waited for limbers. Our
                         18 pdrs fired on the men and scattered them;
                         fire was then directed on the transport. Results
                         could not be observed owing to darkness.

(b) Signals - NIL

(c) Work -
    9 a.m. - 9.30 a.m. about 20 men working in ULSTER TRENCH (U.10.a.)

                                                   Major.
102 B.M.S.   BRIGADE MAJOR
6-1-1918.   102nd (TYNESIDE SCOTTISH) BRIGADE.

PATROLS

1. A patrol of 1 N.C.O. and 4 men left No. 20 Post at 8 p.m. and
   proceeded to enemy wire. From here they turned N and reached a
   point O.28.a.90.50. Here voices could be heard from the enemy
   trench, and a dog barked 5 times. The patrol returned to our lines
   through No.22 post at 10.15 p.m.

2. A patrol leaving No. 17 post at 11 p.m. reports no hostile movement in NO MAN'S LAND.

3. 1 Officer and 8 O.R's left No. 13 Post (O21.b.74.85) at
   8.30 p.m. and proceeded towards the sap at the head of BLOOD LANE
   (O.32.a.14.72). On reaching the enemy wire a detached party went
   forward and carried out an inspection of the wire around the SAP
   HEAD. The following information was obtained -
       (1) No damage has been done to wire by our T.M's.
       (2) The wire has been recently strengthened.
   The patrol returned to our lines at 9.25 p.m.

4. Patrol leaving our lines between Nos 4 and 5 posts reports enemy
   wire at U.1.b.8.6. to be very thick with a large amount of loose wire
   intermingled.

5. Wire from O.32.a.2.2. to 300 yards South of this point was examined by
   a patrol and found to consist of knife rests with loose wire thrown in.
   No gaps were seen

                                                   Major.
                                                   BRIGADE MAJOR.
6-1-18   102nd (TYNESIDE SCOTTISH) BDE.

INTELLIGENCE SUMMARY
102nd (TYNESIDE SCOTTISH) BRIGADE
From 9 am 6-1-18 – 9 am 7-1-18.

WAR DIARY

A. OUR OPERATIONS
1. Machine guns –
    Our Vickers guns fired as follows :–

TIME	TARGET	ROUNDS EXPENDED
6 – 6.30 pm	O.26.d.90.55.	250
10.30 pm – 11 pm	O.26.d.5.8.	250
12.15 pm	Aircraft	100

(ii) Trench Mortars –
   (a) L.T.M.B –
       26 rounds fired at U.1.b.90.63.
       6.30 pm 16 rounds fired at O.32.c.15.35. A hostile M.G. had been located at this point on January 5th.

   (b) 6" Stokes 90 rounds on following targets :–
       BLOCK LANE in O.32.a. (enfilade), U.1.b.85.95., O.32.c.15.35., occasional shots on wire at O.32.a.25.75.
   (c) 9.45" Mortars – 18 rounds on N. end of CHERISY.

(iii) Aircraft –
    Our aircraft were active throughout the day.

B. ENEMY ACTIVITY
(i) Artillery –
    Occasional shells fell on BULLFINCH SUPPORT and SHAWK AVENUE between MALLARD RESERVE and BULLFINCH SUPPORT. The area about O.31.c.25.70. was shelled during the afternoon and damage caused to FIRST AVENUE.

(ii) Trench mortars –
    About 3.30. p.m. 6 heavy minenwerfer fell near WOOD TRENCH.
    At 4.45 p.m. heavy minenwerfer fell on BULLFINCH SUPPORT about O.25.d.6.4.
    A portion of the front line trench between Posts 15 and 16 was blown in by a heavy T.M. shell. A few medium T.M. bombs fell in NO MAN'S LAND" in front of Posts 19 and 20.

(iii) Machine guns –
    On the Right Battalion front Hostile M.G's were very active at morning and evening stand to. Bursts were fired on our front line at intervals during the night.
    On the Left Battalion front hostile M.G's were active during the early part of the night. A hostile gun fired from the enemy front line due East from No. 20 Post.

C. INTELLIGENCE
(i) Movement –
    10 men seen in FONTAINE WOOD at 3 p.m. at 11.30. p.m. our listening post in Sunken road at O.26.a.2.0. saw a hostile patrol of 6 men in front of the enemy wire; they were dispersed by rifle fire..
    Visibility was too bad all day to allow of movement being seen in back areas.
(ii) Miscellaneous –
    Enemy transport heard in direction of FONTAINE WOOD at 7.15 p.m.

102 B.H.Q.
7-1-18.

Major.
BRIGADE MAJOR.
102nd (TYNESIDE SCOTTISH) BRIGADE.

WAR DIARY

INTELLIGENCE SUMMARY
102nd (TYNESIDE SCOTTISH) BRIGADE
From 9 am 6-1-18 – 9 am 7-1-18.

A. **OUR OPERATIONS**
   1. Machine guns –
      Our Vickers guns fired as follows :–

TIME	TARGET	ROUNDS EXPENDED
6 – 6.30 pm	O.26.d.90.55.	250
10.30 pm – 11 pm	O.26.d.5.8.	250
12.15 pm	Aircraft	100

   (ii) Trench Mortars –
   (a) L.T.M.S –
       25 rounds fired at U.1.b.90.63.
       6.30 pm 16 rounds fired at O.32.c.15.35. A hostile M.G. had been located at this point on January 5th.
   (b) 6" Stokes
       55 rounds fired on trenches and dugouts at O.26.d.05.90.,
       O.32.c.95.80., O.26.c.50.82., O.26.c.55.50., ROOF LANE, CHERRY WOOD,
       BLOCK LANE at O.32.a.4.6. – O.32.a.55.55., dugouts and road
       O.32.b.05.50., O.32.a.50. – U.1.b.90.55. – U.20.c.0.8. to
       U.1.b.95.75. O.32.c.55.30. to O.32.c.45.15.
   (c) 9.45" mortars
       50 rounds fired on O.32.b.1.5. – O.32.c.95.80. – O.26.d.0.0.
       O.26.d.8.6. and CHERRY WOOD.

   (iii) Aircraft –
       Our aircraft were active throughout the day.

B. **ENEMY ACTIVITY**
   (i) Artillery –
       Occasional shells fell on BULLFINCH SUPPORT and SHAWK AVENUE between MALLARD RESERVE and BULLFINCH SUPPORT. The area about O.31.c.25.70. was shelled during the afternoon and damage caused to FIRST AVENUE.

   (ii) Trench mortars –
       About 3.30. p.m. 5 heavy minenwerfer fell near WOOD TRENCH.
       At 4.45 p.m. heavy minenwerfer fell on BULLFINCH SUPPORT about O.25.d.6.4.
       A portion of the front line trench between Posts 15 and 16 was blown in by a heavy T.M. shell. A few medium T.M. bombs fell in NO MAN'S LAND" in front of Posts 19 and 20.

   (iii) Machine guns –
       On the Right Battalion front Hostile M.G's were very active at morning and evening stand to. Bursts were fired on our front line at intervals during the night.
       On the Left Battalion front hostile M.G's were active during the early part of the night. A hostile gun fired from the enemy front line due East from No. 20 Post.

C. **INTELLIGENCE**
   (i) Movement –
       10 men seen in FONTAINE WOOD at 3 p.m. at 11.30. p.m. our listening post in Sunken road at O.26.a.2.0. saw a hostile patrol of 6 men in front of the enemy wire; they were dispersed by rifle fire.
       Visibility was too bad all day to allow of movement being seen in back areas.
   (ii) Miscellaneous –
       Enemy transport heard in direction of FONTAINE WOOD at 7.15 p.m.

102 B.H.Q.
7-1-18.

Major.
BRIGADE MAJOR.
102nd (TYNESIDE SCOTTISH) BRIGADE.

To accompany Intell. G. 55

Three patrols went out from the Right Battalion front during the night. The following information was obtained :-

1.. The wire between U.1.b.60.45 and U.1.b.52.60 consists chiefly of knife rests strengthened with loose wire. It forms a good obstacle.

2.. Enemy wire from O.30.c.10.60 to O.32.a.20.12 consists of a strong double apron fence with loose wire, and presents a formidable barrier. Coughing was heard in the sap at O.32.a.20.12.

Two patrols went out from the Left Battalion front -

1.. An Officers and 10 O.R's with a Lewis Gun left No. 15 Post at 6.30 p.m. and took up a position about O.31.b.95.70. A N.C.O. and 2 men then advanced towards the sap at O.32.a.00.77 and saw a hostile patrol of about 15 men who lay down for a short time and then again approached our patrol. Rifle and Lewis Gun fire was opened on the enemy who withdrew hastily, throwing bombs at our men. A party from our patrol was sent to cut off the rearest of the enemy but were unable to do so owing to the rate at which the enemy retired.
Our patrol searched the ground afterwards but could find no identification.
Machine Gun fire was opened on our men from the enemy's line after the hostile patrol had withdrawn. Our party returned at 7.50 p.m.

2.. A patrol of 1 N.C.O. and 4 O.R's left LONE SAP at 1.30 a.m. and report enemy holding a small post about O.32.a.05.90 on the North side of the road, with about 4 men. The post is well wired.

Major.

BRIGADE MAJOR.
7:1:1918.   102nd (TYNESIDE SCOTTISH) BRIGADE.

Intell G. 56

War Diary

INTELLIGENCE SUMMARY
102nd (TYNESIDE SCOTTISH) BRIGADE
From 9 a.m. 7-1-18 - 9 a.m. 8-1-18

A. OUR OPERATIONS
1. Artillery -
Our 18 pdrs were quiet throughout the day. Heavies fired bursts at intervals on back areas.

2. Trench Mortars
(i) L.T.M.B. -
Shoots were carried out on the following targets -

TARGET			ROUNDS
U.1.b.83.30.- "TRENCH JUNCT."	..	..	20
U.1.b.96.79..- "TRENCH JUNCT."	..	..	20
O.26.c.80.65 -		..	30
		Total ..	70 rounds.

(ii) 6" Newtons -

Time.	Rounds.	Target.
11.0 a.m. - 12 noon	20	FORBID TRENCH.
2.30 pm - 3.30 p.m.	25	- do -

(iii) H.T.M.'s -
Between 2.30 p.m. & 4.0 p.m. .... Several H.T.M's were fired on selected targets.

3. Machine Guns -
At 7.15 a.m. our Vickers Guns fired 150 rounds on O.26.d.40.90.

4. Aircraft -
At 3.15 p.m. an aeroplane flew over the enemy's lines. It was not fired on.

B - ENEMY ACTIVITY -
1. Artillery -
Hostile artillery was exceptionally quiet.

2. T.M's -
Active during the morning.

Time.	Target.	Rounds.	Calibre.
10 - 11 a.m.	PIONEER ALLEY.	12	"Pineapples".
9 - 12 a.m.	Front Line of Left Battalion.	-	- do -
-	FOSTER AVENUE	1	H.T.M.
3 - 4 p.m.	Between PIONEER ALLEY and WREN ALLEY........	12	"Pineapples".
		2	H.T.M's.

3. M.G's -
Short bursts at intervals during the night - one gun opposite No. 20 post gave three long bursts of fire on our parapet at 2.30 a.m.

4. Aircraft - Nil.

C - INTELLIGENCE -
1. Movement -
8.45 a.m. Movement in trench at U.1.b.58.60.
9.0 a.m... Flashes from a rifle seen at U.1.b.58.60. smoke rising from this point also.
11.50 a.m. 2 men walking towards crashed aeroplane (U.1.b.) - fired on by our snipers. - one hit claimed.
2.0 p.m... 4 men in MOON QUARRY. (O.33.c.).

/ Signals ..

2.

2. Signals -
   At 4.0 p.m. several

2.

2. Signals -
   At 4.0 p.m. several groups of 4 red lights were fired from enemy line S.E. of LONE SAP.
   About 50 Red rockets were fired at 4.40 p.m. There was no apparent results.

                                                    Major.
                                    BRIGADE MAJOR.
8:1:1918.   102nd (TYNESIDE SCOTTISH) BDE.

                                          To be attached to Intell. G.56

- PATROLS -

1. At 6.0 p.m. a patrol of 1 Officer and 5 O.R's left No. 8 post and patrolled the ground between U.1.b.62.80 and O.31.c.90.40. Hostile patrols were neither seen nor heard.

2. An Officer and 6 O.R's left No. 9,a. post at 9.0 p.m. and reports the wire between O.32.c.10.70 and O.32.c.15.85 is strong and very thick. Coughing in FORRARD TRENCH was heard. The patrol entered our lines at 10.45 p.m.

3. A patrol of 1 Officer and 10 O.R's left No. 15 Post at 6.0 p.m. and proceeded towards the enemy wire around the Sap at the head of BLOCK LANE (O.32.a.13.72).
   On reaching O.32.a.00.70 the patrol halted and one N.C.O. and 4 O.R's advanced to the wire - this was in good condition and no gaps were seen. During this operation the 'flankers' to the main patrol reported a hostile party N.W., and also enemy movement S. of our patrol. After waiting for a considerable time nothing was seen of the enemy, and our lines were entered at 8.15 p.m.
   (There was much hostile rifle and machine gun fire while this patrol was out).

4. One N.C.O. and 4 O.R's left No. 17 Post at 10.0 p.m. and reports the enemy wire at O.26.c.24.25 is in fairly good condition - but several gaps exist. Coughing and talking was also heard.

5. A reconnoitring patrol from No. 19 post saw no signs of the enemy in "NO MAN'S LAND".

                                                Major.
                                    BRIGADE MAJOR.
8 : 1 : 1918.   102nd (TYNESIDE SCOTTISH) BDE.

INTELLIGENCE SUMMARY
102nd (TYNESIDE SCOTTISH) BRIGADE
From 9 am 8-1-18 - 9 am 9-1-18

A. OUR ACTIVITY   (Patrol list attached)
1. Artillery -
   Our artillery activity was normal. Between 9 a.m. and 11.45 a.m. 18 pdrs. carried out an intermittent shoot on FONTAINE WOOD and FONTAINE TR., (U.3.a. - 0.32.c.). At 4.15 p.m. salvoes were fired on the same targets. Harrasing fire was carried out during the night.

2. Trench Mortars -
   (i) L.T.M.'s.
       The following targets were engaged -

   TIME   TARGET   ROUNDS

   2 pm   U.1.b.90.65.   20
   8.45 pm   U.2.a.80.83.   20
   8.45 am   O.32.a.85.80.   20

   (ii) 2" Newtons -
        Between 2 to 3 p.m. 80 rounds were fired on FONTAINE TRENCH and FORWARD TRENCH.

   (iii) M.T.M's -
         40 M.T.M's were fired on FONTAINE TRENCH.

3. M.G's -
   Our Vickers guns fired as follows -

   TIME   TARGET   ROUNDS

   9.30 - 10.30 pm   O.26.d.95.15.   500
   7 - 7.45 pm   - do -   2250
   7.45 - 8.30 pm   O.32.c.78.50.   2250
   9.30 - 10.30 pm   O.32.c.80.41.   - do -

4. Aircraft -
   9.30 a.m.   1 plane over enemy lines not fired on
   9.45 am   1 plane over enemy lines - rifle fire only
   10 am - 1 pm 3 planes over enemy lines - machine gun fire.

B. HOSTILE ACTIVITY
   1. Artillery -   Normal The following trenches were engaged with various calibres at intervals during the day -
      FOSTER AVENUE, Front line near 82 Post, CUCKOO RESERVE, WOOD TRENCH and BROWN SUPPORT. At 4 p.m. 4 gas shells were fired on BROWN SUPPORT. Intermittent counter battery work throughout the night.

   2. T.M's -
      Quiet except for some granatenwerfer activity on Post line.

   3. M.G's -
      Occasional bursts of traversing fire on Post line.

   4. Aircraft -
      Enemy aircraft over our lines at 12.30 p.m. and at dawn.

C. INTELLIGENCE
   1. Movement -
      Abnormal movement in enemy lines during the day.
      (a) Much movement throughout the day, especially between the hours of 9 and 12 a.m. in FONTAINE TRENCH, FONTAINE WOOD, MOON QUARRY & SUN QUARRY. Relief suspected and R.A. informed. There was much sniping on the enemy in FONTAINE TRENCH. 1 hit claimed.
      (b) 11.30 a.m. 3 men digging on parapet of ULSTER TRENCH (O.4.a. & b)

                                                              (c) ...

INTELLIGENCE
Movement - (continued)

(c) Considerable movement in UPTON QUARRY (O.39.c.)
(d) 3.5 p.m. 25 men with full pack left UNICORN TRENCH (U.4.d.) and proceeded towards HENDECOURT.
(e) 3.10 p.m. Boxes about 2 feet long unloaded from pack horse at U.4.c.40.40.
(f) 3.30 p.m. 40 men going towards BURY along BURY - HENDECOURT Road.
(g) Transport on BURY - HENDECOURT Road.
(h) 4 p.m. Limber unloaded at U.5.d.90.20.
(i) 8 a.m. (9-1-18) 30 men working on parapet of ULSTER TRENCH (U.4.a.b.c.)

2. Signals -
A number of single red followed by single green lights were fired from about O.26.b.30.70. No action followed.

for Major.
BRIGADE MAJOR
9-1-18   102nd (TYNESIDE SCOTTISH) BDE.

P A T R O L S

1. A patrol leaving No. 5 Post proceeded to enemy wire at U.1.b.60.70. Whilst examining the belt they were challenged in English ("Halt, who goes there?") from about point U.1.b.72.80. Hostile rifle fire was opened and bombs were thrown. The wire is reported to be from 18 to 24 feet in depth and in good condition. No gaps were found.

2. At 2 a.m. a patrol left No. 7 Post and reports the enemy were very alert. The sap at U.1.b.70.80. is held.

3. A patrol of 1 Officer and 4 other ranks left No. 4 Post and found that the wire between U.1.b.50.85. to sap head at U.1.b.65.82. consist of 3 or 4 belts of knife rests strengthened with loose wire. No gaps were seen. The sap head is wired on both sides and the wire joins with the main belt.

4. A patrol from No. 10 Post reports voices and coughing in FORBARD TR and that the enemy was very alert.

5. A patrol of 1 Officer and 10 O.R. left LONE SAP at 6.30 p.m. and proceeded towards the Sunken Road. There was no enemy post at O.32.a.05.90. (as previously reported). The road is wired with 2 rows of concertina wire. The embankment on both sides is approximately 10 feet high. Several coils of barbed wire were dumped about the road junction (O.32.a.10.85.). Movement could be heard in the sap South of the road. The patrol returned to LONE SAP at 8.15 p.m.

6. A N.C.O's patrol reports the sap at O.32.a.12.10. is occupied.

7. Wire at O.26.c.50.90. is thick, good condition and close to the trench.

Major.
BRIGADE MAJOR.
9-1-1918.   102nd (TYNESIDE SCOTTISH) BDE.

WAR DIARY.

INTELLIGENCE SUMMARY
102nd (TYNESIDE SCOTTISH) BRIGADE
From 9 a.m. 9-1-1918 – 10-1-1918

A. OUR ACTIVITY – (Patrol list attached).

1. **Artillery** –
   Shoots were carried out by our 18 pdrs. on enemy's front line.
   Between 9 a.m. and 12 noon FONTAINE WOOD was intermittently shelled.
   Harrasing fire was carried out on back areas between 7 p.m. and 11 p.m.

2. **Trench Mortars**
   (a) *Light T.M. Bty* –
   The following targets were engaged –

TIME	ROUNDS	TARGET
10.30 am	20	U.1.b.70.10.
1.35 am	20	U.1.b.90.60.
6 p.m.	40	M.G. positions – O.28.a.10.08., O.22.c.50.90.

   (1 hostile machine gun was silenced after this shoot).

   (b) *6" Newtons* –
   50 rounds were fired at intervals on targets in FORWARD and FONTAINE Trenches.

3. **Machine guns** –
   900 rounds were expended between 5.30 p.m. and 8.40 p.m. on Cross Roads at U.2.b.10.20.

4. **Aircraft** –
   5 of our aeroplanes crossed enemy lines at the following times :-
   9 a.m. – plane not engaged.
   9.15 am – 3 planes not engaged.
   9.30 am – 1 plane engaged by A.A. and M.G. fire.
   Four aeroplanes patrolled our line at intervals during the day.

B. ENEMY ACTIVITY

1. **Artillery** –
   Hostile artillery activity reported as follows –

TIME	ROUNDS	CALIBRE	TARGET
–	–	77 mm	Front line (O.31.b.65.5 1 direct hit.
–	–	– do –	Between No. 18 post & WREN ALLEY.
–	–	– do –	BULLFINCH SUPPORT
9.20 am	10	4.2	WOOD TRENCH.
10.15 am	15	4.2	Junction of SWIFT SUPPORT and FIRST AV. (O.31.d.31.40.)
10.30 am	20	77 mm	PIONEER ALLEY.
12 am – 1 pm	–	77 mm	O.31.c.44.70.
2 pm	6	Shrapnel	WOOD TRENCH.

2. **Trench Mortars** –
   Quiet. No activity on Right Bn. front. On the front of the Left Battn. 3 H.T.M's fell about O.26.b.70.35. There was a little granatenwerfer fire on the front line.

3. **Machine guns** –
   Quiet except for usual bursts of fire during the night.

4. **Aircraft** –
   At 10.15 a.m. 2 hostile planes were driven off by A.A. fire.

C. ...

2.

3. INTELLIGENCE
   1. Movement -
      (a) Much movement around SUN QUARRY and STAR CORNER throughout the day.
      (b) 8.10 a.m. - 20 men left UNICORN TRENCH and went in single file towards the DURY - HENDECOURT Rd.
      (c) 11.30 a.m. - 7 men, fully equipped, left CHERRY WOOD (O.22.b.& d) and proceeded South.
      (d) 11.40 a.m. - 9 men entered HENDECOURT along DURY-HENDECOURT Rd.
      (e) 7 a.m. to 8 a.m. - (10-1-18) 100 men in parties of 20 left CHAP'S NEST and moved S.W. along DURY-HENDECOURT Rd.

   2. Transport -
      (a) 8.5 am. A wagon going N on road in U.2.a. stopped and unloaded at O.s.a.45.05. It then proceeded across country to CHAP'S NEST.
      (b) 8.10 am 1 wagon moving S.W. along DURY-HENDECOURT Rd.
      (c) 11.15 am 1 wagon going towards CAGNICOURT on road in
          & V.1.a and b.
          11.35 am

   3. Signals -
      (a) A few green lights were fired by the enemy about 8 p.m. - No apparent action followed.
      (b) 1.15 to 1.30 a.m.- Flashes from signal lamp were observed at approximately P.28.a.10.60.

                                                      Major.
                                                  BRIGADE MAJOR.
10-1-1918.   102nd (TYNESIDE SCOTTISH) BDE.

                        P A T R O L S
                        =============

1. An Officer and 6 O.R's with a Lewis Gun left No. 1 Post at 6.30 pm and proceeded in a S.E. direction to about U.1.b.20.45. After waiting for ½ hour no enemy were seen or heard. Hostile M.G. at U.1.b.68.84. was particularly active.   No 4 Post was entered 7 pm

2. At 8.15 p.m. a patrol of 1 Officer and 4 O.R's left No. 8 Post and obtained the following information -
   (1) The wire between O.1.b.72.20. and O.31.d.95.05. is in good condition and no gaps exist.
   (2) Post at O.31.d.87.00.
   (3) Sap at U.1.b.75.90. was occupied.
   The patrol returned to our lines by No. 7 Post at 10.20 p.m.

3. Patrol from No. 9 post reports wire between points O.32.c.10.85. & O.32.c.15.90. to be thick.

4. A N.CO's patrol leaving No. 13 Post reports that the wire between Gap at O.32.a.15.10. and O.32.a.15.27. is strong - no gaps. Voices in the enemy trench were heard.

5. Wire East of No. 17 Post - O.23.b.30.40. is in good condition. Trench junction at OO.23.c.27.15 is manned.

6. A reconnoitring patrol of 1 N.C.O. and 4 O.R's left No. 20 Post at 10.15 p.m. The wire was examined between points O.26.a.80.10. and O.26.vb.05.30. and found to be very thick except at O.23.a.90.30. The party returned to No. 21 Post at 11.30 p.m.

                                              Major.
102 B.H.Q.   BRIGADE MAJOR.
10-1-1918.   102nd (TYNESIDE SCOTTISH) BRIGADE.

INTELLIGENCE SUMMARY
102nd (TYNESIDE SCOTTISH) BRIGADE.
From 9 am 10-1-18 to 9 am 11-1-18.

A. **OUR ACTIVITY**
  1. Artillery -
       Our 18 pdrs and 4.5 hows were active throughout the period. There was intermittent shelling of enemy trenches - FONTAINE WOOD, SUN QUARRY, and CHERISY-HENDECOURT Road. Salvoes were fired with good results on hostile movement.
  2. Trench Mortars -
       (a) LIGHT T.M's
           Light trench mortars engaged the following targets -

TIME	ROUNDS	TARGET
11.15 am	20	U.1.d.75.95.
2.30 pm	20	U.1.b.94.75.

   (b) H.T.M's
       Between 1 & 3 p.m. several rounds were fired into CHERISY.

  3. Machine guns -
       Vickers guns fired 1200 rounds during the night.

ROUNDS	TARGET
600	U.1.b.10.20. 2
600	0.32.a.55.90.

  4. Aircraft -
       Active. Several planes crossed enemy lines during the morning and early afternoon. At 7.30 a.m. a plane with British markings dropped a light bomb near Right Company Headquarters (O.31.c.20.55.)

B. **ENEMY ACTIVITY**
  1. Artillery -
       Hostile artillery was active on our trench system - especially the Right Sector. The following trenches were engaged -
       SHAFT TRENCH (between's EARL'S COURT and GREY STREET). A direct hit was obtained at junction of SHAFT TRENCH and EARL'S COURT - calibre 4.2. CURTAIN SUPPORT - O.31.c. (77 mm). WOOD TRENCH, 77 mm. Front line (between DODO TRENCH and No. 1 Post). 1 direct hit.

       Between 2 am and 5 am several rounds of various calibres fell near Support trenches. FOSTER CUCKOO, and PELICAN DUMPS were also shelled - no damage reported.

  2. Trench Mortars -
       Some granatenwerfers on Post line - otherwise inactive.

  3. Machine guns -
       Hostile machine guns were very active between 11 p.m. and 1 am on the Right Battalion front. The machine gun at U.1.b.85.65. fired during the night.

  4. Aircraft -
       E.A. crossed our lines at 7.30 am, 11.30 am and 3.15 p.m. They were dealt with by A.A. and M.G. fire.

C. **INTELLIGENCE**
  1. Movement -
       Abnormal movement still prevails behind the enemy's lines.
       (a) There was much movement throughout the day around SUN QUARRY, STAR CORNER, UPTON QUARRY, UPTON WOOD and CROW'S NEST. Parties varying from 5 to 40 men were constantly observed on tracks between the above mentioned places.
       (b) Movement on the DURY-HENDECOURT Rd was large. Parties were seen proceeding in both directions.
       (c) 8.35 am 11-1-18. Smoke rising from N. end of SUN QUARRY. A
       (d) small black chimney is visible here.

(d) -

Movement (continued)

       7.30 am - 8 am - 11-1-18 a great deal of movement in U.3. U.4 U.5, O.32, O.35. About 150 all told were seen moving away from SUN QUARRY, UNICORN and ULSTER trenches. These men were in fatigue dress.

2. <u>Transport</u> -
   (a) 8.10 am 1 wagon going N.E. on BURY-HENDECOURT Rd. in U.11.b.
   (b) 4 p.m. to 4.30. Transport moving in a Northerly direction on Roads in O.35.c. and U.4.b.
   (c) 8 am 11-1-18, 1 wagon with a white cover proceeding N.E. on BURY-HENDECOURT Rd.

2. <u>Signals</u> - NIL

3. <u>Miscellaneous</u> -
   6.5 am enemy bombed his own wire opposite No. 4 Post.

P A T R O L S

1. A patrol leaving No. 2 Post at 8 p.m. reports that the enemy's wire at U.1.b.60.50. is strong, and no gaps were seen.

2. Wire between O.32.c.2.0. and O.32.c.1.8. was examined by a patrol from No. 10A Post. The wire was good and consisted of knife rests with loose wire intermingled. No gaps were found.

3. A N.C.O's patrol from No. 12 Post reports that the enemy wire E of this post is in good condition, consisting of concertina and knife rests.

4. Wire at O.26.c.20.10. and O.26.a.70.14. is thick.

5. Protective patrols report no unusual activity on the part of the enemy.

                                                       for Major.
                                                  BRIGADE MAJOR

11-1-1918   102 nd (TYNESIDE SCOTTISH) BRIGADE.

Intel G.61

INTELLIGENCE SUMMARY
102nd (TYNESIDE SCOTTISH) BRIGADE
From 9 am 12-1-18 to 9 am 13-1-18

A. OUR ACTIVITY (Patrols attached)

1. Artillery -
Enemy trenches and CHERISY were subjected to bursts of fire at frequent intervals during the day. Between 1 - 3 pm back areas were also shelled.

2. Trench Mortars -
(a) L.T.M.B. -
The following targets were engaged -

10.30 am	15 rounds	U.1.b.25.30.
11.30 am	26 rounds	O.32.a.55.80.
2.45 pm	15 rounds	U.1.b.94.75.

(b) 6" Newtons -
Between 11 am and 2 pm a number of rounds were fired into CHERISY and enemy trenches W of CHERISY. 3 direct hits were obtained on FONTAINE TRENCH about O.32.c.60.30.

3. Machine guns -
Between 5 - 7 pm our Vickers guns fired 3750 rounds on CHERRY BRIDGE, O.32.b.98.45. Between 9 - 10 p.m. 500 rounds were fired on tracks in O.32.c.

4. Aircraft -
Our aircraft was active during the morning and early afternoon.

7 am - 9 am (13-1-18) 9 planes over enemy lines.
9 am - 11 am 5 planes over enemy lines/our
11 am - 12 am 4 planes patrolling enemy lines
2 pm - 2.30 pm 4 planes over enemy lines.
3.30 pm 4 planes over enemy lines.

B. ENEMY ACTIVITY -

1. Artillery -
The following trenches were intermittently shelled -

Front line between Posts 1 and 4 (77 mm)
CURTAIN SUPPORT (4.2)
FOSTER AVENUE - N.29.b. (4.2) 2 direct hits.

The area around FOSTER CUCKOO DUMP and BROWN DUMP was also shelled - no damage reported. There was slight hostile shelling of back areas during the night.

2. Machine Guns -
Intermittent firing on Post line during hours of darkness.

3. T.M's -
Slight activity in vicinity of DODO and SWIFT Trenches - chiefly Granatenwerfer.

4. Aircraft -
Enemy 'planes were over our lines at 11.0 a.m. and 2.30 p.m.

C. INTELLIGENCE -

1. Movement -
Movement in this Sector is still slightly above normal -

(a) 8.30 a.m. Small parties of men all wearing fatigue dress left UNICORN TRENCH, ULSTER TRENCH (U.4.c.) and SUN QUARRY. It is probable that these parties work on the BURY-HEUDECOURT Rd.

/ (b) 10.10 a.m.

- 2 -

C. INTELLIGENCE -

1.. Movement - continued)

(b) 10.10 a.m.   Much movement to and from SUN QUARRY.

(c) 10.30 a.m.   20 men left CROWS NEST and proceeded N.E.
                 along DURY-HENDECOURT Rd.

(d)   Considerable individual movement in O.32.b.

2.. Transport -

(a) 8.10 a.m.   Wagon unloaded at U.8.b.90.40.

(b) 3.30 p.m.) 2 wagons moving S.E. on the DURY-HENDECOURT
    5.30 p.m.) Road stopped at O.N.d.70.08. They were
                 shelled by our artillery, causing them to
                 return quickly before being unloaded.

3.. Signals .. NIL.

4.. Work -
    O.32.a.42.50)   New earth on parapet for
    O.32.a.52.70)   40X and 60X respectively.

         It is reported that work is being done in U.9.b.
    Old timber and new earth can be seen. A man was levelling
    earth down around U.9.b.05.55.

5.. Miscellaneous -
    (1).. 10.10 a.m. 77 m.m. battery located at U.11.a.75.80.
          R.A. informed. One direct hit observed on
          right gun pit of battery.

    (2).. hostile T.M. firing from U.2.d.40.30.

                                                        Major.
                                              BRIGADE MAJOR.
13 : 1 : 1918.   102nd (TYNESIDE SCOTTISH) BRIGADE.

                                        To accompany Intell. G. 61

                        —   P A T R O L S   —

    Five reconnoitring patrols were sent out during the night.
The enemy wire was reported on and found to be in good condition.
(previous patrol reports confirmed).

    Dawn patrols were also out.   A hostile patrol was seen leaving
O.32.a.20.40. and moved Southwards keeping close to his own
lines. Fire was opened on them by our patrol and they immediately
withdrew.
                                                          Major.
13 : 1 : 1918.   BRIGADE MAJOR
                                     102nd (TYNESIDE SCOTTISH) BDE.

INTELLIGENCE SUMMARY
102nd (TYNESIDE SCOTTISH) BRIGADE
From 9 am 13-1-1918 to 9 am 14-1-1918

A. OUR ACTIVITY

1. Artillery –

During the period our artillery was more active than usual – aeroplanes co-operated.

Shoots were carried out on enemy trenches, FONTAINE WOOD, SUN QUARRY, and the CHERISY-HENDECOURT Road. Back areas were shelled intermittently throughout the night, and counter battery work took place.

2. Trench Mortars –

(a) L.T.M.'s.

The following shoots were carried out –

11.30 am	15 rounds	U.1.b.80.29.
12.7 pm	20 rounds	O.32.a.45.40.
3.30 pm	16 rounds	U.1.b.94.73.

(b) 6" Newtons –

11.30 am	15 rounds	FONTAINE WOOD
2.30 pm	–	Enemy trenches.

(c) H.T.M's –

2 – 4 pm	20 rounds	CHERISY

3. Machine Guns –

Vickers guns expended 2000 rounds on the following targets –

11 – 12 pm	500 rds	Tracks (U.2.a.)
6 – 7) 9 – 9.30) pm	1500 rds	Cross roads O.32.b.50.95.

4. Aircraft –

There was much air activity throughout the day. From 7.30 am – 4 pm our planes were crossing enemy lines at frequent intervals.

At 10 am 12 aeroplanes in groups of 3 were observed well over hostile trenches.

B. ENEMY ACTIVITY

1. Artillery –

9 – 11 am	20 (77 mm)	Post line
9 – 11 am	10 (4.2)	N.30.d.1.3.
10 am	6 (5.9)	CURTAIN SUPPORT
12 am – 1 pm	8 (4.2)	Near PELICAN DUMP (N.36.b.3.6.)
3 – 3.30 pm	6 (4.2)	– do –
8 – 8.30 pm	8 (4.2)	– do –
7 & 10 pm	20 (4.2)	FOSTER CUCKOO DUMP.

There was intermittent fire throughout the night on the Support line area.

2. T.M's –

Between 9 am – 2 pm about 20 granatenwerfers fell on Post Line in O.26.a. & c.

3. Machine guns –

Intermittent fire during the night

4. Aircraft –

Several attempts were made by E.A. to cross our lines during the morning, but were unsuccessful.

2 p.m. 5 E.A. over our lines for 15 minutes.

3.15 pm E.A. engaged by one of our planes and was driven down behind enemy lines.

C. **INTELLIGENCE**
   1. Movement -

8.5 am	3 men moving in trench at U.1.b.62.85. Trenches shallow at this point, and appears to be damaged by T.M's.
8.10 am	Smoke rising U.2.d.20.60.
9.15 am	Timber taken into SUN QUARRY.
10.30 am	16 men going towards DURY on DURY-HENDECOURT Rd.
11.30 am	5 men going towards HENDECOURT on DURY-HENDECOURT Rd.
11.45 am	Movement around UPTON WOOD.
12.5 pm	12 men approaching stack of timber at P.31.c.80.25. Returned and entered UPTON WOOD.
2.40 pm	Movement around CROW'S NEST.
-	Dugout at U.2.b.20.65. - men entering, smoke rising, guard changes every hour.

   2. Work -

10.10 am	Men working on new dugout. (O.25.c.30.50)
3.20 pm	Men working at P.31.c.80.20.
-	Much new work in U.10.c.

   3. Transport -

4 p.m.	A wagon moving S.E. along DURY-HENDECOURT Rd. - engaged by artillery. A second wagon stopped in U.6.b. when our 18 pdrs fired. - thought to be waiting for darkness.

   4. Signals -   NIL

PATROLS

There were no hostile parties seen or heard in "NO MAN'S LAND" during the night.

DAWN PATROLS report no unusual hostile activity.
4 Reconnoitring patrols were sent out and the following reports were made on the condition of the wire.

   (1) Enemy wire between O.32.c.1.5. and O.32.c.15.90. was continuous. No gaps could be found.
   (2) Between O.32.a.15.20. and O.32.a.10.60. the wire is in good condition.
   (3) Enemy wire from O.32.a.10.30. to O.32.a.10.70. is good and no gaps were found.
       Sounds of revetting could be heard from O.32.a.20.53.
   (4) Wire was also good between O.26.c.50.90. and O.26.a.60.10.

102 B.H.Q.
14-1-18

for Major.
BRIGADE MAJOR
102nd (TYNESIDE SCOTTISH) BDE.

INTELLIGENCE SUMMARY
102nd (TYNESIDE SCOTTISH) BRIGADE.
From 9 am 14-1-1918 - 9 am 15-1-1918

A. OUR ACTIVITY
1. Artillery -
Shoots were carried out on enemy trenches, FONTAINE WOOD and CHERISY. From 7.50 pm to 8.10 pm and at intervals during the night CHERRY BRIDGE, OTTER LANE, hostile approaches in O.32.d. and CHERISY were shelled by 18 pdrs. and 4.5.hows.

2. Trench Mortars.
(a) M.T.M.B.
The following shoots were carried out:-
3 pm   35 rds   Trench and dugouts O.26.c.55.40.
                    to O.26.c.30.60.
3.10 pm)
3.20 pm) 15 rds   O.32.a.55.8.0.

(b) 9" Newtons -
At 3 p.m. 20 rounds were fired on FORWARD TRENCH

3. Machine guns -
5600 rounds were expended by our Vickers guns during the night.

7 - 8 pm   600 rds   ) O.26.d.70.40.
11.15 pm - 5 am 5000 rds.   (U.2.b.10.20. roads in
                             (O.26.c. and O.32.b.
                             (CHERRY BRIDGE

4 Aircraft -
Slight activity only. At 2.25 pm one of our planes crossed enemy lines and was not engaged.

B. ENEMY ACTIVITY
Hostile artillery activity was again below normal. The following were the targets engaged - CURTAIN SUPPORT, FOSTER AVENUE, (N.30.a.c & d) BULLFINCH SUPPORT, SHARK AVENUE, and PELICAN Dump,
Six (4.2) were fired into HEMINEL during the afternoon.

2. Trench mortars -
Very slight activity. At 11.15 am M.T.M. fired 4 rds. from O.26.c. on to WREN ALLEY. There were a few granatenwerfer bombs on the post line.

3. Machine Guns -
No machine gun activity during the day, and only occasional bursts during the night.
Hostile M.G. fired from about O.26.b.10.28..

4. Aircraft - NIL.

C. INTELLIGENCE
1. Movement -   VISIBILITY INDIFFERENT
(a) 2 pm   Head and shoulders of men at U.3.b.60.55. - were shelled by 18 pdrs
(b) 2.30 pm 2 men carrying water from U.2.b.3.3. to U.2.a.90.10. This operation was repeated 5 times in 30 minutes.
(c) 4 pm   A party of about 100 men moved S through O.3.b. and d. Owing to the poor visibility it was impossible to see what they were wearing.
(d) 4 pm   4 men loitering about in Sunken Rd. (U.3.b.40.65.)
1 man is posted as a sentry and faces S.W. (This has continued for 2 days)

2. Transport -
4 p.m.   3 large and 4 small wagons moved S.W. on the DURY - HENDECOURT Rd. First stop was at U.6.b.70.20. A small party of men gathered round the wagon then moved off to HOP TR. (U6d) carrying bags.

2 wagons...

2 wagons stopped at U.5.d.70.10. and 2 proceeded across country to UPTON TRENCH (U.5.b.10.15.)

3 wagons also moved from U.6.c. to U.4.b.25.60. - no parties approached to unload (The transport was shelled at different points but no damage was observed)

3. Signals - Nil.

PATROLS

1. An Officers patrol from No 9 post reports sap at O.32.a.14.11. was occupied. The wire between O.32.c.15.75. and O.32.a.15.00 thick, and no gaps.

2. Wire between U.1.b.55.50. and U.1.b.70.75. was low and deep A petrol engine could be heard behind the enemy's lines

3. Enemy wire around U.1.b.70.80. was in good condition.

4. The following information was obtained from a patrol leaving No. 21 Post at 6.30 pm :-

    (1) Wire about O.26.a.80.20. consists of an apron fence with concertina and loose wire. No gaps could be found.

    (2) The sap at O.26.a.65.10. was occupied. A rifle grenade and 4 very lights were fired from here.

    (3) There was no trace of the enemy in NO MAN'S LAND

5. Patrols from Nos. 15 and 16 Posts report the enemy to be very alert. He bombed his wire at frequent intervals.

102 B.H.Q.
15-1-1918.

for Major.
BRIGADE MAJOR.
102nd (TYNESIDE SCOTTISH) BDE.

INTELLIGENCE SUMMARY
102nd (TYNESIDE SCOTTISH) BRIGADE.
From 9 am 15-1-18 to 9 am 16-1-18

A. OUR ACTIVITY

1. **Artillery** -
Enemy trenches, CHERISY and back areas were subjected to frequent bursts of fire.
Harassing fire was carried out during the night on C.T's, roads and tracks.

2. **Trench Mortars** -
   (a) L.T.M.'s -
   The following targets were engaged -

10.50 am	15 rds	U.2.a.60.70.
12.45 pm	20	0.32.a.55.20.
2.50 pm	(10	0.25.c.43.70.
	(10	0.26.b.03.15.

   (b) 6" Newtons -
   At 11 am 20 rds. were fired on FORWARD TRENCH.

3. **Machine guns** -
During the hours of darkness our Vickers guns fired 5500 rds. on

1.	FORK ROADS	C.27.c.3.9.	5000 rds.
2.	" "	U.8.b.40.35.	500 rds

4. **Aircraft** -
No activity reported.

B. ENEMY ACTIVITY

1. **Artillery** -
Hostile artillery activity was below normal.

   CURTAIN SUPPORT, WOOD TRENCH, and FOSTER CUCKOO DUMP (O.25.c.) were lightly shelled at intervals.
   At 3 pm about 6 gas shells fell near O.25.c.75.95.

2. **Trench mortars** -
There was a slight increase in hostile trench mortar activity.
The following is reported

1.30 pm	7 L.T.M's	BULLFINCH SUPPORT
2 to 2.45 pm	10 M.T.M's	SWIFT SUPPORT (3 failed to detonate)
7 pm	2 M.T.M's	- do -

   Throughout the day a considerable number of granatenwerfer bombs were fired on the post line - especially on Left Battn. Front.

3. **M.G's** -
Quiet except for usual short bursts of fire throughout the night.

4. **Aircraft** - NIL

C. INTELLIGENCE

1. **Movement** -
Poor visibility hindered good observation.
   (a) 9.10 am — 4 men left trench at U.2.c.05.70. and entered SUN QUARRY.
   (b) 2 pm — 2 men left SUN QUARRY and walked towards STAR CORNER (O.34.a.)
   (c) — Smoke issuing from suspected dugout at U.8.b.40.65. (Movement seen here for past 5 days).
   (d) — There is a heap of new chalk at U.2.c.50.40. Night work is done at this point for the pile is larger every morning.

(e) ......

Movement (continued)

        (c) 7 - 8 am   Men loitering about ULSTER TRENCH
                         (U.4.a. and c)

(b) Transport -
    (a) 7.15 am   Wagon unloaded by 6 men at U.4.b.90.40.
    (b) 4.15 pm   2 limbers moving S.W. along BURY -
                         HERDECOURT RD. 1 stopped at U.5.c.60.45.
                         (having cut across country)- the other at
                         U.5.d.65.05)

(c) Signals -   NIL

P A T R O L S

1. A patrol leaving No. 4 Post reports a hostile post at
U.1.b.85.30. Very lights were fired from this point but no
movement was heard. The wire in this vicinity was good and
no gaps were observed.
    The sunken rd. (ROTTEN ROW) was examined in a few places.
It was found to contain portions of a light railway track.
No hostile parties were encountered.

2. 5 other reconnoitring patrols went out from our lines
during the night. Progress was hampered by the condition of
the ground.
    Coughing was heard in many parts of the enemy's front line,
but no hostile patrols were seen.

3. DAWN PATROLS have nothing unusual to report.

                                              Major.
                                       BRIGADE MAJOR
102 B.H.Q.
16-1-18   102nd (TYNESIDE SCOTTISH) BRIGADE.

INTELLIGENCE SUMMARY
102nd (TYNESIDE SCOTTISH) BRIGADE
From 9 am 16-1-18 to 9 am 17-1-18

A. OUR OPERATIONS
   1. Artillery -
      Intermittent shelling took place on hostile trenches, CHERISY, and back areas.
      C.T's and roads were subjected to harassing fire throughout the night.

   2. Trench Mortars -
      (a) L.T.M.B.
         30 rounds were fired on trench junction at 0.26.d.25.99.

      (b) 6" Newtons
         20 rounds were fired on FORRARD TRENCH.

      (c) H.T.M's
         30 rounds were fired on FONTAINE WOOD.

   3. Machine Guns - NIL.

   4. Aircraft - Nil

B. ENEMY ACTIVITY
   1. Artillery -
      There was no shelling of the front and support trenches on either sub-sector.
      10 5.9's on FIRST AVENUE, near Right Battn. H.Q. (W.36.b.43.02) and 6 H.E. shrapnel shells burst over PELICAN DUMP (W.36.b.30.60.)
      From 4 p.m. till midnight, WANCOURT and the area between WANCOURT and HENINEL was subjected to a slow rate of fire - calibre chiefly 4.2

   1ᴬ - Gas - A few gas shells on EGRET TRENCH at 12.30 p.m.

   2. T.M's -
      Hostile mortars were inactive. At 1.35 p.m. 2 H.T.M's fell near WREN ALLEY. A few granatenwerfers were also fired on to BULLFINCH SUPPORT at 11.45 am.

   3. M.G's -
      Usual short bursts of fire. Hostile M.G's were active apparently from SAP at 0.26.a.65.10., 0.26.b.10.30. and from trench junction at 0.26.c.80.70.

   4. Aircraft -
      NIL.

C. INTELLIGENCE
   1. Movement -
      (a) 9.45 am   14 men in marching order proceeding N.E. on road in 0.34.a.
      (b) 10 am   2 men laying wires from ULSTER TRENCH (U.4.c.80.70.) through U.3.d. and c, and were lost to view behind FONTAINE LES CROISILLES. The wire runs close to OUSE TRENCH on the Southern side.
      (c) 10.10 am   3 men carrying timber approximately 8' long 4" by 4" from CHERISY - HENDECOURT RD (0.33.d.15.10.) to ULSTER TRENCH 0.34.d.20.05.
      (d) 9 am - 10.30 am   Several small parties walked across from FONTAINE to ULSTER TRENCH U.4.a.70.20.
      (e) 10.25 am   7 trucks on right railway at V.14.c.10.45. At 3.20 pm 6 had gone, - 1 still remained at dark. One truck appeared to have a large crane and another loaded high with timber.
                                                                    (f) ....

Movement (continued)

  (f) 2 pm 3 men working on parapet of CRUX TRENCH
         (U.9.c.60.90.) This work went on till dark.
  (g) 4 pm Smoke rising from U.2.d.20.70.
  (h)   Sentry again seen in Sunken Road
         U.8.b.40.65.

2. Transport -
 There was the usual amount of transport on the DURY, HENDECOURT RD. from 3.30 p.m.
 Our artillery greatly hampered their progress.

3. Signals -
 1.45 p.m Enemy signalling from CROWS NEST.

4. Miscellaneous -
 1. Puffs of smoke as from a gun at U.11.a.75.80.
 2. Sniping - 2 hits claimed by our snipers on enemy in FORRARD and FONTAINE TRENCHES.

PATROLS

 4 reconnoitring patrols went out during the night. The following information was obtained -

  1. Enemy wire between U.1.b.80.98. and O.32.c.10.25. in good condition - no gaps were found.
  2. Enemy heard repairing his trenches.
  3. Talking in FORRARD TRENCH.
  4. Sap at O.32.a.15.11 was occupied.
  5. Hostile machine gun at O.26.c.45.70.
  6. No hostile patrols were seen or heard in NO MAN'S LAND.

102 B.H.Q.   Major.
17-1-1918   102nd (TYNESIDE SCOTTISH) BRIGADE MAJOR.
                BRIGADE.

INTELLIGENCE SUMMARY
102nd (TYNESIDE SCOTTISH) BRIGADE
From 9 am 17-1-18 to 9 am 18-1-18

A. **OUR ACTIVITY**
   1. **Artillery** -
      Less active than usual. 18 pdrs fired occasional salvoes on SUN QUARRY (O.32.c.), FONTAINE WOOD, and enemy support trenches.
      Harassing fire was carried out during the night on hostile roads and tracks.

   2. **Trench Mortars** -
      (a) **L.T.M.B.** Nil.

      6" Newtons and M.T.M's fired on selected targets in U.1.b., U.2.a. and O.32.a.

   3. **Machine guns** -
      Vickers guns fired 4000 rounds on the following targets -

10.30 pm and 11.30 pm	2000 rds.	O.27.c.30.90. (Fork Rds.)
10.30 pm and 1.30 am	2000 rds.	CHERRY BRIDGE

   4. **Aircraft** - Nil.

B. **ENEMY ACTIVITY** -
   1. **Artillery** -
      Below normal in the forward area. WANCOURT was shelled at intervals throughout the day and night (calibre 10.5 cm).

5.30 pm to 6 pm	10 rds (10.5 cm)	THE NEST (N.30.a.30.20.)
9.55 pm	3 rds. (")	PELICAN DUMP. (N.36.b.82.67.)

   2. **Trench Mortars** -
      The following hostile T.M. activity is reported -

10.30 am	12 granatenwerfers	In rear of Nos. 20 & 21 Posts.
3.30 to 4.15 pm	15 H.T.M's (4 blind)	Around O.31.b.40.84
4.30 pm	8 M.T.M's	FOSTER AVENUE about O.25.d.70.20
5.30 am	12 granatenwerfers	Near Nos. 20 & 21 Posts.

   3. **Machine guns** -
      At 8.30 pm hostile M.G's were very active on the front line posts of the Left Subsector. Occasional bursts were fired during the night.
      A machine gun appeared to be firing from Sap (O.26.c.40.68.)

   4. **Aircraft** - NIL

C. **INTELLIGENCE**
   1. **Movement** - Visibility poor during the morning.

2.30 pm	4 men left SUN QUARRY and proceeded towards STAR CORNER.
2.30 to 3.40 pm	Men working on parapet of CREW TRENCH (U.9.c.)
3.30 to 4 pm	4 men carried stretcher and Red Cross flag from SUN QUARRY and disappeared in Sunken Rd. O.35.a.1.9.
3.40 pm	15 men walking from UPTON TRENCH (U.8.a) to UNICORN TRENCH (U.4.b)
3.50 pm	20 men in fatigue dress left SUN QUARRY and disappeared about O.35.a.

      During the afternoon

Movement (cont) - During the afternoon men were again seen in SUNKEN ROAD at U.8.b.40.65.

(2) Transport -

 3.35.p.m.   8 Wagons moving S.W. along DURY-HENDECOURT ROAD. 2 Wagons stopped at U.6.b.60.10 and were met by a small party of men from HOP TRENCH. The remaining 4 wagons proceeded across country and halted at U.6.a. 50.50. (Heavies opened fire causing the wagons to return N.E. along DURY-HENDECOURT ROAD)

 4.10.pm   1 Wagon moved from behind UPTON WOOD proceeding S. on road in U.6.b. and d.

 7.25.am   1 Wagon standing at U.6.b.95.55.

 7.40.am   1 " " " OGRE PIT- U.5.c.

(3). Miscellaneous.- Smoke arising from U.2.a. 20.50.

(4). Signals. - Nil.

PATROLS.

Protective Patrols. - were out during the night and report no signs of the enemy in "NO MAN's LAND".

Dawn Patrols. - report no unusual hostile activity.

18-1-1918.

for Major,
BRIGADE MAJOR,
102nd (TYNESIDE SCOTTISH) BDE.

WAR DIARY

INTELLIGENCE SUMMARY
10th (JAMAICA SCOTTISH) BRIGADE
From 6 am 15-1-18 to 6 am 16-1-18

A. OUR OPERATIONS
1. Artillery -
Bursts were fired at intervals by 18 pdrs. on enemy support line in O.32.a. and c, OTTER LANE, FONTAINE WOOD and CHEMIN. At 3.15 pm 4.5 hows shelled HUN and BOOM Quarries for a period of five minutes. There was also intermittent fire on back areas.

2. Trench Mortars -
(a) L.T.M's: Nil
(b) 6" Newtons carried out a small shoot on enemy trenches between 3 and 4 p.m.

3. Machine Guns -
Intermittent fire was kept up on enemy lines during the night.

4. Aircraft -
There was increased activity during the morning and much flying was done over enemy's lines. At 11 am one of our planes, flying low, fired on to CHEMIN. Hostile A.A. was below normal.

B. ENEMY ACTIVITY
1. Artillery -
Hostile artillery activity was slightly above normal on the right subsector and normal on the left.

```
   9 am      30 rds.    10.5 cm       N.36.Central.
   9.15 am   6 rds       "            O.31.c.3.8.
   10 am     6 rds       "            N.30.d.20.75.
    "        18 rds      "            Near No. 1 Post
   10.30 am  12 rds      "            DODO TRENCH
   10 - 12
   noon.     40 rds     77 mm         Between front line & SWIFT SUPPORT
   1 pm      8 rds      10.5 cm       N.36.Central
   3.40 -
   4.30 pm   30 rds     77 mm         Between front line & SWIFT SUPPORT
   4.15 pm ( 6 rds      10.5 cm
           ( 12 rds     77 mm.        Junction of FIRST AVENUE and
                                      CUSTARD SUPPORT.
   8 - 10 pm  Back areas and PELICAN CAMP were shelled with 10.5 cm shells
   10 pm     4 rds.     10.5 cm.      TANK TRENCH.
```

FOSTER CUCKOO CAMP and HINDENBURG CAMP were shelled during the afternoon.
Hostile fire was maintained on our lines at a slow rate until 2 am.

2. M.G's -
Increased activity. Bursts were fired on our wire and an intermittent fire was kept up on our post line during the hours of darkness.

3. T.M's -
Inactive.

4. Aircraft -
E.A., flying very high crossed our lines on 3 occasions during the morning.

C. INTELLIGENCE
1. Movement -

8.20 am   20 men in fatigue dress moved from O.15.a. and
               disappeared into trench at O.4.d.30.10.

                                                              8.30 am ..

Movement (continued)

8.20 am	3 men in fatigue dress around SUNQUARRY.
10.40 am	20 men moving along railway from U.4.d.25.10. to U.10ga.
7.15 am – 8 am (19-1-18)	40 men on parapet of ULSTER TRENCH (U.10.a.)

There was much individual movement throughout the day.

2. Transport –

8.10 am	1 wagon going S.E. on BURY-HENDECOURT Rd. in U.6.b.
8.35 am	Wagon unloaded at U.6.b.70.20. – appeared to be road material.
3.45 pm	Wagon halted at U.6.b.70.20. – a party from HOP TRENCH proceeded to this spot.
4 pm	3 wagons moving S.W. along BURY-HENDECOURT Rd. halted in U.6.b. Darkness prevented further observation
7.40 am & 7.55 am (19-1-18)	2 wagons stopped at U.6.b.95.20.

3. Work –
Digging operations were observed at O.31.d.85.00. at 11.30 am and 3.15 pm

4. Signals –
About midnight 6 green and 6 red lights were fired by the enemy from the front line in O.32. No apparent action followed.

5. Miscellaneous –
12.30 pm 3 gun flashes observed at point U.11.d.10.65.

P A T R O L S

RECONNOITRING PATROLS
1. Enemy wire between O.32.c.15.25. and O.32.a.10.70. was examined and found to be in good condition.
2. A patrol of 2 N.C.O's and 3 men left LONE SAP at 11 p.m. and reports that the enemy wire around O.26.c.20.10. is thick and strong. A machine gun was active from the direction of the trench junction at O.26.c.25.12.
3. A patrol leaving our lines between Nos. 18 and 19 Posts proceeded along the Sunken rd for a distance of 150 yds. No signs of the enemy were seen or heard during 30 minutes wait.

DAWN PATROLS Report no unusual activity.

PROTECTIVE PATROLS were out from dusk till dawn. No enemy were seen, but work was in progress in hostile lines.

Major.
BRIGADE MAJOR.
102 B.H.Q.
19-1-18.   102nd (TYNESIDE SCOTTISH) BRIGADE.

INTELLIGENCE SUMMARY
102nd (TYNESIDE SCOTTISH) BRIGADE
FROM 9 am 19-1-18 to 9 am 20-1-18

WAR DIARY

A. OUR ACTIVITY
1. **Artillery** -
During the day our artillery kept up a harassing fire on enemy back area. Several small working parties were dispersed. The following targets in the forward area were engaged by our guns and hows:
Enemy front and support lines, SUN QUARRY, OTTER LANE, FONTAINE les CROISILLES and FONTAINE WOOD.
Harassing fire was carried out by 18 pdrs. throughout the night.

2. **Trench Mortars** -
(a) Stokes - At 2 p.m. 30 rds. were fired on trench junction and dugouts at C.23.d.29.90.
(b) 6" Newtons - 10 rds. were fired on FONTAINE TRENCH about C.23.c.55.90. at 8.30 am

3. **Machine Guns** -
Vickers guns fired as follows -
2500 rounds .... RAILHEAD C.23.d.95.15.
3000 rounds .... CHERRY BRIDGE C.22.b.95.45.

4. **Aircraft** -
Active throughout the day. Several formations of 4 machines flew over enemy lines frequently.
Hostile A.A. fire was very poor.

B. ENEMY ACTIVITY
1. **Artillery** -
Hostile artillery was less active than on previous day -

9.30 am	4 rds.	10.5	TANK TRENCH
9.50 - 10.30am	18 rds	10.5 cm	Between Right Bn. H.Q. and PELICAN DUMP. 3 direct hits were obtained on Sunken Rd. close to PELICAN DUMP causing some casualties

FOSSE COOKOO DUMP was also shelled periodically.

2. **Trench Mortars** -
Quiet on the Right front, fairly active on the left.

9a - 9.30 am   10 H.T.M's   Near junction of SWAN ALLEY and SWIFT SUPPORT

(It is reported that these bombs had fins and to resemble our own H.T.M.)

2.35 pm   5 M.T.M's   Junction of SNYKER ALLEY & BULLFINCH SUPPORT.

There was a certain amount of grenatenwerfer activity along our post line.

3. **Machine Guns** -
Intermittent fire during the night. One gun was active on the sunken road near PELICAN DUMP.

4. **Aircraft** -
1 E.A. at a great height crossed our lines at 11.45 am.

INTELLIGENCE -

C. INTELLIGENCE
1. Movement -
The usual [illegible] movement of small parties was again observed around SUB QUARRY, STAR CORNER, UPTON WOOD and UPTON QUARRY. Many parties were dispersed by our artillery.

8.30 am		30 men round CHALK PIT (O.8.c.).
8.45 am	5 men)	All wearing full packs were observed walking Eastwards from FONTAINE WOOD.
10 am	6 men)	
10.10 am	10 men)	
10 am	....	7 men in marching order left CROWS NEST and proceeded N.E. along BURY-HENDECOURT RD.

2. Transport -

3.30 pm	Wagon unloaded at P.31.d.10.50.
4.5 pm	2 wagons at 5 mins. interval moving S.W. were unloaded at U.6.b.90.50. - then returned.
4.30 pm	At dusk a line of transport wagons (about 7) could be seen on the BURY-HENDECOURT Rd. in U.6.b. moving S.W.
7.10 & 8 am	2 wagons moving N.E. on BURY-HENDECOURT Rd. in U.6.b.

3. Signals -
(a) A red light was fired from enemy front line in O.23.c. at 2.15 am. No apparent action followed.

(b) Left Battn. reports searchlight was flashing from the direction of TRIANGLE WOOD at 7.20 pm.
Right Battn.- A searchlight was observed in the direction of VIS-EN-ARTOIS at 8.15 pm.

4. Miscellaneous -

9.40 - 10.35 am.	Puffs of smoke were observed from hostile battery at U.4.b.30.20. Before firing men were put out on both flanks apparently to prevent individuals from passing in front of guns. (Artillery informed).
10.40 am	14 men working on this Battery position.

PATROLS

1. Enemy wire at O.32.a.10.70. was good. No movement was heard in gap N of this point.

2. Wire at O.26.c.20.80. was also in good condition. Voices were heard in enemy's front trench.

3. A N.C.O's patrol from No. 12 Post reports wire from U.26.a.60.05. to O.26.a.88.50. to be thick and in good condition.

DAWN AND PROTECTIVE PATROLS saw no signs of the enemy.

for Major.
BRIGADE MAJOR.

102 B.B.Q.
20-1-18
102nd (TYNESIDE SCOTTISH) BRIGADE.

WAR DIARY.

INTELLIGENCE SUMMARY.
102nd (TYNESIDE SCOTTISH) BRIGADE
From 9 am 30-1-18 to 9 am 31-1-18

A. **OUR OPERATIONS**

1. **Artillery** -
During the day 18 pdrs fired on enemy's front and support trenches, CHERISY and FONTAINE WOOD. Back areas were engaged by our heavies at frequent intervals.

2. **Trench Mortars (L.T.M.B.)**
At 5 p.m. 40 rounds were fired on trench junction and dugouts at O.34.d.55.30.

3. **Machine Guns** -
Vickers guns expended 800 rds. on s.o.s. and 8000 rounds on the following targets -

    (a) 3000 rds   Cross Roads O.32.b.49.92.
    (b) 5000 rds   Fork Roads and tracks O.57.c.35.90

4. **Aircraft** -
Our aeroplanes were active throughout the whole of the day. On many occasions flights were made well over hostile lines. There was little hostile fire.

B. **ENEMY ACTIVITY**

1. **Artillery** -
Hostile artillery activity was confined chiefly to back areas. ADINKEL was subjected to intermittent fire throughout the day.
FIRST AVENUE, CONCRETE RESERVE, FOSTER AVENUE and PELICAN KEEP also received attention.

2. **T.M's** :
Inactive. Several granatenwerfer bombs were fired on No. 17 Post at 7.30am

3. **M.G's** -
Bursts were fired at frequent intervals on the Post line. Hostile guns appeared to be active from saps at O.32.a.18.90. and O.32.a.15.10.

4. **Aircraft** -
Hostile planes were more active than usual. Many attempts were made to cross our lines but were frustrated by our fire.

C. **INTELLIGENCE**

1. **Movement** -
Movement was again seen round GUN QUARRY, FONTAINE WOOD, UPPER QUARRY, UPPER WOOD and CROWS NEST. A great proportion of the men observed were in fatigue dress.

2. **Transport** -

  7.15 am   A wagon moving S.W. along BURY-HENDECOURT Rd. stopped and unloaded at U.6.b.95.30.

  7.20)
  7.30)   a.m. 31-1-18. Transport moving in both directions on the
  7.35)   BURY-HENDECOURT Rd at these times.
  7.40)

3. **Miscellaneous** -
(1) 1 p.m. and 4 p.m. Puffs of smoke seen from a gun firing at V.3.c.40.80.
(2) A box loophole can be seen at S.11.b.80.80.

4. **Signalling** -

4. Signalling -
7.20 am Signalling from CROWS NEST.

PATROLS

1. An Officers patrol reports that the wire between U.1.b.80.95. and 0.32.c.10.28. is thick and no gaps were visible. Coughing was heard in FORRARD TRENCH.

2. Wire between 0.32.c.15.30. and 0.32.a.20.20. is very strong and appears to be very thick.

3. A N.C.O's patrol left No. 12 post at 11.40 pm and proceeded to the enemy wire at point 0.32.a.10.40. The belt was found to be in good condition. A hostile machine gun fired from gap at 0.32.a.20.12. and a dog (thought to be in NO MAN'S LAND) was heard barking N of the patrol. No hostile parties were seen or heard.

4. Wire between 0.26.c.15.00 and 0.26.c.35.50. was examined and found to be continuous and in good condition.

5. A patrol leaving No. 21 Post found the enemy wire between 0.26.a.20.10. and 0.26.a.20.30. in good condition, continuous and plentiful. No signs of the enemy were seen in NO MAN'S LAND.

102 B.H.Q.
21-1-1918.   102nd (TYNESIDE SCOTTISH) BRIGADE.
BRIGADE MAJOR.

WAR DIARY

INTELLIGENCE SUMMARY
102nd (TYNESIDE SCOTTISH) BRIGADE
From 9 am 21-1-1918 to 9 am 22-1-18

A. **OUR ACTIVITY**

1. **Artillery** -
   18 pdrs. fired on enemy trenches, FONTAINE WOOD, SUN QUARRY, MOON QUARRY, UPTON TRENCH and CHERISY.
   Back areas were subjected to intermittent fire throughout the period.

2. **Trench Mortars** -
   (a) L.T.M.S -
   At 11 am 20 rounds were fired on dugouts between O.26.c.60.50. and O.26.c.80.65.
   (b) 6" Newtons -
   20 rounds were fired at 2.50 p.m. on selected targets in U.2.a.

3. **Machine guns** -
   Vickers guns engaged the following targets -

   (a) 5000 rounds   O.27.d.15.80.
   (b) 2000 rounds   U.3.b.15.81.

4. **Aircraft** -
   Our planes were very active during the day especially between the hours of 9 and 12 a.m. Several of our formations crossed enemy lines At 11.10 am and 3.30 pm machine guns were fired into enemy trenches.
   Hostile a.a. guns were quiet.

B. **ENEMY ACTIVITY**

1. **Artillery** -
   Hostile artillery fire was normal.
   The following activity is reported -

   6.30 am - 11.30 am   ....   Intermittent shelling of area N.36.b. - calibre, chiefly 77 mm.

   10 am - 1.30 am   ....   LARK LANE and N.36.c. lightly shelled.

   11 am - 1 pm   ....   30 (77 mm) shells - EGRET LOOP.

   QUARRY DUMP was shelled periodically.

1A. **Gas** -
   A few gas shells were fired on THE NEST at 6.30 p.m. Between 10 - 11 pm about 5 gas shells fell North of SENSEE (N.23.b.3.3.)

2. **T.M's** -
   Slight activity on the Right Subsector, quiet on the Left.

   9.30 - 10 am   16 L.T.M.   ground No. 7 Post (mortar located at O.32.c.55.60., artillery informed).
   2.30 pm   6 granatenwerfers Junction of FIRST AVENUE and Front line (O.31.d.60.15.).

3. **M.G's** -
   Increased activity. Frequent bursts were fired on Post line throughout the night.
   Hostile guns fired from O.32.c.60.50. and O.33.a.12.42.

4. Aircraft.

4. **Aircraft** -
Two hostile planes crossed our lines at 11.25 am and were engaged by A.A. guns.

C. **INTELLIGENCE**

1. **Movement** -
Movement still continues around FONTAINE WOOD, SUE QUARRY, UPTON QUARRY, UPTON WOOD and CROWS NEST.
Many parties were dispersed by our artillery.
There has been considerable indirect movement on the top of trenches which points to the fact that hostile trenches are in bad condition.

2. **Work** -
(1) 9.10 am — 20 men working in UNICORN & ACOL, S.M.C.
(2) Throughout the day work was in progress on the PUM-LECHECOURT RD. 18 N.31.c.

3. **Dumps** -
1. More material (timber and wire visible) has been added to the Dump at U.5.c.30.90.
2. Timber has been dumped during the night at U.5.d.80.95.

4. **Transport** -
Transport again seen on PUM-LECHECOURT RD.

5. **Signals** -
1. Enemy fired 4 red rockets from front line in O.25.a. at 5 pm. No apparent action.
2. 7 am — Lamp signalling active from CROWS NEST.

6. **Miscellaneous** -
10.25 am .... 5 puffs of smoke were seen from hostile battery in U.4.b.30.20.
2.30 pm .... Smoke again seen from this battery. Artillery informed and fire was opened on this spot. The fifth shell set fire to an ammunition dump close to the guns. Smoke and flames continued for 45 minutes. Men were then observed throwing earth upon it. The battery was silenced - 10 direct hits were observed.

PATROLS
----

1. The sap at U.1.b.71.85. was occupied. Bombs were thrown into the sap and the garrison retaliated. The sap has a belt of wire in front but does not continue round the sides. Much 'shuffling' was heard in FORWARD TRENCH.

2. Enemy wire astride the sunken road in U.1.b. is good - no gaps were found. Wire at O.26.c.15.30. was strong and thick. Coughing was heard in FORWARD TRENCH.

3. Wire between O.27.a.30.45. and O.27.a.85.10. was examined and found to be in good condition.

4. A R.S.F's patrol from No. 12 Post reports :-

   (a) Enemy wire between O.27.a.15.X. and O.32.a.10.30. in good condition - no gaps were seen.
   (b) A working party was heard in FORWARD TRENCH - O.27.a.
   (c) No enemy patrols encountered in NO MAN'S LAND

                                        [signature]
                                           Major.
                                    for BRIGADE MAJOR.
108 B.K.S.   103rd (TYNESIDE SCOTTISH) BRIGADE.
23-1-1916.

INTELLIGENCE SUMMARY
102nd (FIFESHIRE SCOTTISH) BRIGADE
From 0 am 22-1-18 to 23-1-18

A. OUR OPERATIONS

1. **Artillery** –
During the day 18 pdrs engaged enemy front and support trenches, FONTAINE WOOD and GUENISY. Back areas were intermittently shelled. Hostile parties were also engaged with good effect.

2. **Trench Mortars** –
   (a) L.T.M's –
   Between 11 am and 1 pm 45 rounds were fired on an active hostile L.T.M. (O.22.c.80.90.) One direct hit was obtained.

   (b) 6" Newtons –
   Trenches in O.1.b. and O.32.a. were engaged.

3. **Machine guns** –
Vickers guns expended 6000 rounds on the following targets –

   4000 rounds .... CHERRY BRIDGE (O.33.b.98.45.)
   2000 rounds .... RAILHEAD (O.23.d.95.15.).

4. **Aircraft** –
Much activity throughout the day. Machine guns were fired into enemy trenches.

B. ENEMY ACTIVITY

1. **Artillery** –
Hostile artillery activity was below normal on the forward area. Rearward areas were intermittently shelled.
The following trenches were subjected to fire – CURTAIN and BULLFINCH SUPPORT trenches, BRET LOOP and BRET TRENCH. The area around HINDENBURG DUMP (T.6.b.6.0.) was shelled at frequent intervals.

2. **T.M's** –
No activity on right subsector, normal on the left.

   9 and 10 cm   6 light minenwerfer   CURTAIN SUPPORT
   9.30 cm   4 H.T.M's   Front line (O.25.d.).

Granatenwerfer bombs were fired on the Post line.

3. **A.A's** –
Much activity against our aircraft during the day – usual short bursts at night – no particular target.

4. **Aircraft** –
NIL.

C. INTELLIGENCE

1. **Movement** –
Movement of small hostile parties was again observed in U.2.a. & b, O.35.c., O.35 and U.11.b.

   8 – 9 am   ..... Small enemy working party in front line
                      trench (O.1.b.) dispersed by L.G. fire.

   12.35 pm   ..... Timber carried from dump at U.6.c.30.80.
                      to UNICORN TRENCH (U.6.d.).

Transport –
Transport was observed on DURI – MARCOING RD & GUENISY – MARCOING RD. at dusk and between 7 and 8 am.

Signals – NIL.

PATROLS

1. A N.C.O's patrol reports FORWARD TRENCH probably held by M.G. and rifle posts. No movement was heard in this trench and no hostile parties were encountered.

2. Enemy wire around O.32.a.15.95. consisted of 3 belts of double apron fence with concertina and portable obstacles at intervals <u>in front</u> of the forward belt. No gaps were found and the enemy was very alert.

3. The following points were obtained by a patrol leaving LONG SAP.

   1. Sap at O.32.a.15.95. is held. Very lights were fired from it occasionally.

   2. Sap head is protected by a thin belt of wire behind which is a much stronger belt.

   3. Talking in NARROW TRENCH was heard.

   No hostile parties were seen in NO MAN'S LAND.

4. Wire between O.32.a.10.40. and O.32.a.10.55. was examined by a N.C.O's patrol from No. 12 Post and is reported to be

   (i) Good
   (ii) Thick
   (iii) Without gaps.

5. A patrol leaving No. 10 Post was challenged by an enemy sentry from O.26.c.20.73. Six stick bombs were thrown at our patrol and immediately fire was opened in the direction of the enemy post. Hostile wire was then examined between O.26.c.40.70. and O.26.a.30.10. and found to be -

   (i) Good condition
   (ii) Plentiful.
   (iii) Gap 3" wide at approximately O.26.c.40.70.

   (signature) 2/Lt
   BRIGADE MAJOR
   102nd (TYNESIDE SCOTTISH) BRIGADE.

23-1-1918.

INTELLIGENCE SUMMARY
102nd (TYNESIDE SCOTTISH) BDE.
From 9 am 23-1-18 to 9 am 24-1-18

War Diary

A. OUR OPERATIONS
  1. Artillery -

   Enemy trenches and FONTAINE WOOD were shelled intermittently by 18 pdrs. Between 6 - 9 am and 10 am - 12 noon back areas were engaged. Sniping of movement continued throughout the day.

  2. Trench mortars -
   (a) L.T.M.B. -

11 am	15 rds	Suspected M.G. emplacement (U.1.b.08.65)
12.15 & 3.30 pm	60 rds	Dugouts, O.32.a.50.70.

   (b) 6" Newtons - fired 20 rds. on enemy front line between 2 & 4 pm
   (c) M.T.M's expended 30 rds. on selected targets.

  3. Machine guns -
   Vickers guns fired as follows during the night -

2000 rds.	Tracks O.32.d.36.25.
2000 rds.	River Crossing U.2.b.85.85.

  4. Aircraft -
   Line patrols were active during the morning.

B. ENEMY ACTIVITY
   Hostile artillery was active throughout the day. The following is reported -

6 - 8 am	20 rds	(4.2)	Back area (N.29)
8.45 am	30 rds	(77 mm)	SWIFT SUPPORT
10 - 12 am	20 rds	(4.2)	Back area (N.29)
2 - 3 pm	12 rds.	(4.2)	CUCKOO PASSAGE (N.26.b.)
5 - 5.30 pm	16 rds.	(77 mm)	Vicinity of Bn. H.Q. (N.26.b.6.1.)
1 am	15	(77 mm)	SWIFT SUPPORT

   FOSTER AVENUE, FOSTER CUCKOO DUMP and PELICAN DUMP were shelled at intervals - 1 direct hit on FOSTER AVENUE.

  2. T.M's -
   Increased activity.

8 am	3 H.T.M's	(Between Nos. 6 and
8 - 9 am	6 - do -	(8 Posts.
		(Between front line
		(and CURTAIN SUPPORT
		((O.31.b.)
2 - 4.15 pm	18 - do -	(Around O.31.b.7.7. &
		(O.25.d.7.1.
		(2 direct hits on
		(FOSTER AV. & 1 hit on
		(LONE SA.
5 pm	9 - do -	(SWIFT SUPPORT.

   Granatenwerfers were also fired on the Post line of the Left Sub-sector.

  3. Machine guns -
   Occasional bursts of fire on Posts.

C. INTELLIGENCE

C. INTELLIGENCE
  1. Movement –
     Much individual movement.
     8 am ...   Considerable movement around large dump at U.5.c.30.20
                Men carried timber from dump to U.10.d.

  2. Transport –
     No transport was observed before dusk.
     8 am ...   A wagon drawn by 4 horses moving S.E. on CHERISY –
                KHREJOUKI Rd (J.13.b.)

  3. Enemy sniping posts –
     1. U.1.b.80.30. Active at 8.45 am (23-1-18), 7 – 8 am (24-1-18)
     2. O.25.c.12.30. Active throughout the day.

  4. Signals –
     9.25 pm .....   4 green lights were fired from FORWARD TRENCH
                     (O.26.c.) Immediately the enemy fired rifle
                     grenades and throw bombs into his wire about
                     O.25.a.20.15.

  5. Miscellaneous –
     1. Fish bombs were again fired from hostile M.T.M's.
        A bearing was taken on a mortar from O.26.d.5.47 and found to
     be 129° TRUE. (No opportunity arose for a second bearing to be
     taken).
     2. Enemy bombed his wires at intervals during the night about
     O.1.b.7.2.
     3. A hostile wiring party was heard about O.33.c.10.30. Lewis
     gun fire was opened and sounds of work ceased.

                          P A T R O L S
                          =============

  1. An Officer's patrol from No. 14 Post reports enemy wire between
      O.32.a.10.30. and O.32.a.10.70. in good condition. The belt
      consists of knife rests and concertina wire- 2'0" to 5' high.
      Nothing was seen or heard of the enemy.

  2. A N.C.O's patrol reports wire across the sunken road in O.25.c.
      to be good,- consisting of knife rests. Coughing was heard in
      NARROW TRENCH at O.26.c.45.65.

      Protective patrols were sent out from the Right Sub-sector. No
                  signs of the enemy were seen.

      Dawn patrols report no unusual enemy activity.

                                                    BRIGADE MAJOR.
  24-1-1918.   102nd (TYNESIDE SCOTTISH) BDE.

INTELLIGENCE SUMMARY
102nd (I.B.) Brigade.
From 9.a.m. 24.1.18. to 9.a.m. 25.1.18.

A. OUR OPERATIONS

1. <u>Artillery</u> - The following targets were subjected to frequent bursts of fire throughout the day - FONTAINE WOOD, CHERRY WOOD, SUN QUARRY, OTTER LANE and enemy front and support trenches.
   Harrassing fire was carried out during the night on hostile roads and tracks.

2. <u>Trench Mortars</u> -
   (a) <u>L.T.M.B</u> - Nil
   (b) <u>6" Newtons</u>. -7.30. - 9.30.a.m. 20 rds. were fired on suspected T.M.positions in CHERISY.
       At 11.a.m. about 30 rds. were fired on trench junction at C.32.c. 18.55.
   (c) <u>M.T.Ms</u>. expended 15 rds. on enemy dugouts.

3. <u>Machine Guns.</u> -
   Vickers Guns fired 5,000 rds. during the hours of darkness.
   <u>Targets</u> - (a) FORK ROADS, C.27.c.50.90. .... 3,000 rds.
             (b) NEW WORK & TRACKS, C.33.a. .... 2,000 "

4. <u>Aircraft</u> -
   Considerable activity during the morning and early afternoon. On several occasions our 'planes were observed flying over enemy lines. - There was little hostile A.A.fire.

B. ENEMY ACTIVITY -

1. <u>Artillery</u> - Hostile artillery was less active than on preceding day.
   The following is reported -

9.30.a.m.	6.rds. (4.2)	Between SWIFT SUPPORT and FRONT LINE
11.0.a.m.	8.rds. (77 mm)	Between POSTS 7 and 10 C.31.d.
12.30.a.m.	2 rds. (4.2)	C.31.c. 45. 79.
2.0.p.m.	- (77 mm)	No.12 POST and CURTAIN SUPPORT

   Dumps were shelled intermittently throughout the night.

2. <u>T.M.s.</u> Slight granatenwerfer activity on post line.

3. <u>M.G's.</u> - Quiet. A few bursts throughout the night.

4. <u>Aircraft</u> - 6.e.a. were observed flying high over their own lines at 3.40.p.m. No attempts were made to cross our lines.

C. INTELLIGENCE. -

1. <u>Movement.</u>
   Considerable individual movement prevails behind enemy lines.

8.5.a.m.	9 men with full kit proceeding N.E. on DURY-HENDECOURT RD. (U.6.b).
8.10.a.m.	6 men working on parapet of USHER TRENCH (U.10.d)
8.25.a.m.	15 men left CROWS NEST and were lost to view behind UPTON WOOD.
10.40.a.m.	2 men carrying timber from DUMP U.3.b.70.10 to ULSTER TRENCH C.34.d.

   Movement....(cont)

-(2)-

Movement (cont)

1.15.p.m.   10 men carrying timber from DUMP U.5.c.30.20.
to ULSTER TRENCH (U.4.c.)

2. MISCELLANEOUS

11.30.p.m.   Enemy bombed his own wire at 0.32.c.10.60
Enemy post located at 0.32.a.2.9. (Men seen entering and leaving)

PATROLS.

A. RECONNOITRING PATROLS.

1. An officers patrol leaving No.17.a. POST (0.25.d.90.60)
reports enemy wire between 0.26.c.30.40. and 0.26.c.40.60
in good condition - consisting chiefly of double apron
fencing and concertina.
    No hostile patrols were seen.

2. A large enemy wiring party was seen at 0.26.c.55.98 by
a patrol of 1 N.C.O. and 4 men. Lewis Gun and rifle fire
was opened on to this spot. The patrol again
reconnoitred, but no trace of the enemy could be found.
Hostile wire E of 19 and 20 POSTS reported to be thick
and in good condition.

3. A N.C.O. and 3 men left No.12 POST at 2.a.m. Another
hostile wiring party was seen at 0.32.a.20.20. This
information was reported to Lewis Gunners. Fire was
brought to bear on party causing them to disperse.
    A reconnaissance of the wire was then made,
which was found to be in good condition.

B. DAWN PATROLS report no unusual enemy activity. Two of
the enemy were seen returning to their own lines E
of No.12 POST. Fire was opened on them.

C. PROTECTIVE PATROLS. were sent out from the right subsector and nothing was seen of the enemy.

                                              2/Lt
                                    Major,
                                BRIGADE MAJOR,
25-1-1918.   102nd (TYNESIDE SCOTTISH) BDE.

INTELLIGENCE SUMMARY
102nd (TYNESIDE SCOTTISH) BRIGADE
From 9 am 25-1-1918 to 9 am 26-1-1918

A. OUR ACTIVITY

1. **Artillery** -
   Increased activity. Harassing fire was kept up during the day by 18 pdrs. on FONTAINE WOOD, SUN QUARRY, OTTER LANE, CHERRY WOOD, CHERISY and enemy front and support lines. Hostile trenches were also shelled at intervals during the night.

2. **Trench Mortars** -
   (a) L.T.M.B.
   The following shoots were carried out -

   9.45 am ..... 27 rounds .... Trench and dugouts between
   O.26.c.5.45. and O.26.c.80.60.

   2.30 pm ..... 34 rounds .... O.26.b.25.00.

   3.15 pm ..... 40 rounds .... Dugouts, U.2.a.40.55.

   (b) 6" Newtons fired 20 rounds on enemy defences at 1.30 pm

3. **Machine guns** -
   Vickers machine guns engaged the following targets during the night -

   4000 rounds .... CHERRY BRIDGE
   1000 rounds .... Turning point O.26.d.75.40.

4. **Aircraft** -
   Good visibility enabled our aircraft to do much useful work. Both scout and artillery machines were active over our own and enemy lines during the day.

B. ENEMY ACTIVITY

1. **Artillery** -
   At 7.45 pm harassing fire was directed against our front system for 10 minutes - otherwise hostile artillery was inactive on the forward area.

   9.10 am .... 12 rds (4.2) .. FIRST AVENUE(S.36.b)
   8 pm .... 6 rds (4.2) .. - do -
   8.35 pm .... 4 rds(all blind) PELICAN DUMP
   9.45 pm .... 4 rds - do - - do -

   At 6 am 2 rds (4.2) were fired on Sunken Road N.22.d.40.40. (One direct hit).

2. **T.M's** -
   Hostile mortars were very active between 8.30 am and 11 am. The following activity is reported -

   8.30 am .... 6 L.T.M's ..... E. of our wire.
                                    (O.31.b.35.10.)
   9.15 am .... 4 light minenwerfers. In rear of No. 4 Post
   9.30 am 8   - ditto -   Around O.31.d.4.40.
   10 am   6   - ditto -   In rear of posts 2 & 4
   11 am   1   - ditto -   Junction of FIRST AV.
                                    & SWIFT SUPPORT.

   There was considerable T.M. activity between Nos. 15 and 16 Posts. (One direct hit on front line).

   / 3. Machine guns ..

3. Machine guns -
   Short bursts of fire throughout the night - no special target

4. Aircraft -
   Activity above normal. R.A. crossed our lines at 8 am,
   10.30 am and 2 pm. At 7.20 pm an aeroplane (thought to be
   hostile) crossed our lines flying Eastwards.

C. INTELLIGENCE
   1. Movement -

   9.45 am .... 10 men working on parapet of UNICORN TR.
                       (U.4.b.)

   10.20 am .... 4 men carrying timber from dump at
                       U.3.c.30.20. to ULSTER TRENCH.

   The usual individual movement was again observed around
   CHERRY WOOD, FONTAINE WOOD, SUN QUARRY, and UPTON WOOD.

   2. Smoke - issuing from U.3.d.80.85. and U.4.b.70.35.

   3. Signals -
   At 5.30 pm enemy burst 4 shrapnel shells over his front line.
   Immediately a white light was fired and the artillery ceased.

                       P A T R O L S

   RECONNOITRING PATROLS

   1.   A patrol of 1 Officer and 5 other ranks left No. 14 Post
        at 3.30 am and proceeded Eastwards to the enemy wire. Nothing
        was heard of the enemy and no hostile parties were seen. No. 18
        Post was entered at 4.30 am.

   2. PROTECTIVE PATROLS were out from dusk till dawn and report no
      signs of the enemy.

   3. DAWN PATROLS report no unusual hostile activity.

                                                    Major.
                                            BRIGADE MAJOR.
   24-1-1918   102nd (TYNESIDE SCOTTISH) BRIGADE.

WAR·DIARY·
H·Q· 1º2 · INFANTRY · BDE·

February 1918.

Army Form C. 2118.

WAR DIARY
or
~~INTELLIGENCE SUMMARY.~~
(Erase heading not required.)

HQ 102 Inf. Brigade. February 1918

Instructions regarding War Diaries and Intelligence Summaries are contained in F.S. Regs., Part II. and the Staff Manual respectively. Title pages will be prepared in manuscript.

Volume 27

Place	Date	Hour	Summary of Events and Information	Remarks and references to Appendices
M.36.C.8.0. Sheet 51B.S.W.	1st		Orders received to disband 20th NF and 21st NF. 1st Bn. E. Lancs Regt. moved into DURHAM LINES and was placed at disposal of G.O.C 102nd Inf. Bde. for work.	
"	2nd		Orders issued to 20th NF and 21st NF to be disbanded. 600 men furnished today and were HENINEL switch. 100 men provided today for VI Corps Hospitals	
"	3rd		20th and 21st NF disbanded. Transport 20th NF was attached to Bde. HQ. HQ. 20th and 21st NF moved to BLAIREVILLE Camp. 25th NF joined 102nd Inf. Bde and was accommodated in DURHAM LINES. Work on HENINEL switch (600 men) and keeping cable (100 men) continued.	
"	4th		Work on HENINEL switch and keeping cable continued.	
"	5th 6th		Work on HENINEL switch and keeping cable continued.	
"	7th		OO 190 issued. 400 men provided to work on HENINEL switch, 100 for keeping cable.	Appendix 1(a)
BLAIREVILLE	9th		102nd Brigade Group marched in accordance with OO 190. Bde HQ opened at BLAIREVILLE on arrival at 12 noon.	

Army Form C. 2118.

Instructions regarding War Diaries and Intelligence Summaries are contained in F. S. Regs., Part II. and the Staff Manual respectively. Title pages will be prepared in manuscript.

WAR DIARY
or
INTELLIGENCE SUMMARY.
(Erase heading not required.)

Feb. 1916 HQ 102 Inf. Brigade

Place	Date	Hour	Summary of Events and Information	Remarks and references to Appendices
SOUYEN-ARTOIS	10th		Brigade Group marched in accordance with OP.190. B.M. 142 opened at CHATEAU at 2-0 p.m. EN ARTOIS on arrival at 12 noon.	
AMBRINES	11th		Brigade Group marched in accordance with OP.190. Bde HQ opened at Mayor's House AMBRINES on arrival at 12 noon.	
"	13th to 26th		Training continued.	
"	26th		102 Brigade was inspected by the Corps Commander at AMBRINES at 3 pm. OP. 191 issued.	Appendix 1(A)
"	27th		102nd Brigade Group marched in accordance with OP. 191. Bde HQ opened at Mayor's House POMMIER at 5-30pm.	Issued
POMMIER	28th		102 Brigade Group marched in accordance with special order B OP 191. Bde HQ opened at HAMELIN COURT at 2pm.	Appendix 2 Appendix 3

Authentic Report attached
Concluded

[signature]
Brigadier General
Cmdg 102 Inf. Bde.

Appendix ......

CASUALTIES.

FEBRUARY 1918.

OFFICERS.   N I L.

OTHER RANKS.

	Killed.	Wounded.	Missing.
25th Bn. North'd. Fus.	-	2	-
102nd L.T.M.B.	-	1	-
	-	3	-

Appendix 4

HONOURS and AWARDS.

FEBRUARY 1918.

N I L.

Appendix 1

OPERATION ORDERS.

WAR DIARY appendix 1(b)
of
Late B.Mns

SECRET.   Copy No. 16

Ref. Map   102nd INFANTRY BRIGADE ORDER NO... 191.
Sheets 51c
and 51b 1:40,000
LENS 11, 1:100,000.   26.2.1918.

1..   54th Division is to take over the Centre Sector,
        VI Corps Front on night 1/2nd and 2/3rd March, relieving
        178th Inf.Bde., 59th Division in Right Section and 8th
        Inf. Bde. of 3rd Division in Left Sections.
                102nd Inf. Bde. will relieve 178th Inf.Bde. in
        the Right Section on night 2/3rd March.

2..   102nd Brigade Group will march to the BOISLEUX
        (late GOMIECOURT) area on Feb. 27th and 28th in
        accordance with the attached Tables 'A' and 'B'.
                Orders for the relief in the line will be issued
        later.

3..   Each Unit after passing the starting point will
        halt automatically at 10 minutes to each clock hour, and
        resume the march automatically at each clock hour.

4..   Lieut. Colonel S.A.ACKLOM, D.S.O.,M.C., will
        command 102nd Brigade Group on the march on Feb.27th.

5..   Arrival in billets and position of H.Q. will be
        reported by each Unit of the Group to Brigade Head-
        quarters each day.

6..   Reports during the march to the head of Column.

        ACKNOWLEDGE.
                                            K. Lobridge.
                                                Major,
                                            BRIGADE MAJOR,
                                         102nd INFANTRY BRIGADE.

Issued at 10.30p to -

                G.O.C............................Copy No. 1.
                Brigade Major.................... "   "   2.
                Staff Captain.................... "   "   3.
                Bde. Signals..................... "   "   4.
                Bde. Transport Officer........... "   "   5.
                Transport Off. 20th N.F.......... "   "   6.
                22nd Battn. N.F.................. "   "   7.
                23rd Battn. N.F.................. "   "   8.
                25th Battn. N.F.................. "   "   9.
                102 L.T.M.Bty.................... "   " 10.
                206th Field Coy. R.E............. "   " 11.
                102nd Field Amb.................. "   " 12.
                No.3 Coy Div. Train.............. "   " 13.
                Bde. Supply Officer.............. "   " 14.
                Camp Commandant, 54th Divn....... "   " 15.
                Diary and File................... Copies Nos.16 & 17
                H.Q. 54th Division............... Copy No.18.

MARCH on FEB. 27th. 1918.   TABLE A.   To accompany O. O. No. 191.

Serial No.	Troops in order of March	Starting Point Place	Time of passing	ROUTE	DESTINATION	REMARKS.
1	Bde. H.Q. 102 L.T.M.B. Transport 20th N.F. (less detached vehicles)	Road Junction I.3.d.7.2.	8.30 a.m.	GIVENCHY LE NOBLE - AVESNES LE COMTE - BARLY - BAVINCOURT - LA CAUCHIE.	Bde. H.Q. and 20th N.F. t'port POMMIER. 102 L.T.M.B. BIENVILLERS (Sheet 11 LENS)	Bde. H.Q. closes at AMBRINES at 8.0 a.m.
2	25th N.F.	Road Junction I.3.d.7.2.	8.33 a.m	As for Bde. H.Q.	BERLES AU BOIS	300x in rear of above.
3	22nd N.F.	Road Junction I.3.c.1.3.	8.35 a.m	AMBRINES thence as for Bde. H.Q.	BERLES AU BOIS	300x in rear of 25th N.F.
4	23rd N.F.	Road Junction I.4.b.9.9.	9.7 a.m.	Road Junction I.11.c.5.5. thence as for Bde. H.Q.	POMMIER.	After road junction I.11.c. to be 300x in rear of 22nd N.F.
5	208th Field Co. R.E.	Cross Roads I.5.c.1.7.	9.19 am	Road Junction I.11.c.5.5. thence as for Bde. H.Q.	HUMBERCAMP.	300x in rear of 23rd N.F.
6	102 Field Ambulance	Cross Roads I.5.a.1.7.	9.27 am	Road Junction I.11.c.5.5. thence as for Bde. H.Q.	BIENVILLERS.	300x in rear of 208th Field Co. R.E.
7	Mounted portion of Div. H.Q.	Point where road enters wood I.31.c.2.0.	9.30 am	AVESNES LE COMTE thence as for Bde. H.Q.	HUMBERCAMP.	To join column at AVESNES LE COMTE and be 300x in rear of 102nd Field Ambulance.
8	No. 3 Co. Div. Train less baggage wagons.	Road junction LIENCOURT. I.32.c.1.9.	9.45 am	AVESNES LE COMTE thence as for Bde. H.Q.	BIENVILLERS.	300x in rear of ltd. portion of Div. H.Q.

Addressed all Recipients of O.O. 191 :-

Reference O.O.191, herewith Table 'B' for move to-morrow the 28th inst.

Acknowledge.

27: 2: 1918.

P Brough
for
Major,
BRIGADE MAJOR,
102nd INFANTRY BRIGADE.

Ref. Map. Sheet 11 LENS.   TABLE B   March on Feb. 28th 1918.   To accompany O.O. 191.

Serial No.	Troops in order of march.	Starting Point. Place	Time of passing	ROUTE	DESTINATION.	REMARKS.
1	22nd N.F.	Cross roads immediately N. of 1st B in BERLES AU BOIS.	8.30 a.m.	MONCHY AU BOIS - ADINFER - AYETTE BOURGELLES LE COMTÉ.	BELFAST CAMP ERVILLERS.	
2	25th N.F.	ditto	8.40 a.m.	ditto	INNISKILLING CAMP ERVILLERS.	300x in rear of 22nd N.F.
3	Bde. H.Q., T'port 20th M.F. less detached vehicles 102 L.T.M.B.	Road junction ¼ mile S. of P in POMMIER.	8.20 a.m.	BIENVILLERS AU BOIS - MONCHY AU BOIS - thence as for 22nd L.F.	HAMLINCOURT.	Bde.H.Q. closes at POMMIER at 7.45 a.m. after MONCHY AU BOIS to be 300x in rear of 25th N.F. 102 L.T.M.B. joins column on passing through BIENVILLERS AU BOIS.
4	23rd N.F.	ditto	8.28 am	ditto	CLONMEL LINES HAMLINCOURT.	300x in rear of 102 L.T.M.B.
5	208th Field Co. R.E.	POMMIER Church.	8.30 a.m.	ditto	HAMLINCOURT.	300x in rear of 23rd N.F.
6	Mtd. portion of Div. H.Q.	POMMIER Church.	8.38 am	As for Bde. H.Q.	GOMMECOURT.	300x in rear of 208th Field Co. R.E.
7	102nd Field Ambulance.				Train Camp at BIENVILLERS AU BOIS.	Remains at BIENVILLERS AU BOIS.
8	No. 3 Coy. Div. Train less Baggage wagons				Train Camp BOISLEUX AU MONT.	To march independently in rear of column and to clear ADINFER by 11.30 a.m.

SECRET.   appendix 1(a)   Copy No.. 16

Ref. Map.
Sheet 11
LENS.

102nd INFANTRY BRIGADE ORDER No ... 190.

7 : 2 : 1918.

1.. The 34th Division (less Pioneer Battalion) is being relieved in Corps Reserve and is to move into the LE CAUROY area.
34th Division passes into G.H.Q. Reserve at noon February 9th.

2.. 102nd Brigade Group will march on February 9th., 10th, and 11th to the MILAINES area in accordance with the attached Tables 'A', 'B' and 'C'.

3.. Each Unit, after passing the starting point, will halt automatically at 10 minutes to each clock hour and resume the march automatically at the clock hour.

4.. Arrival in billets and position of Headquarters each day will be reported by all Units of the 102 Brigade Group to Brigade Headquarters.

5.. Reports during the march to the head of the Column.

Acknowledge.

Major,
BRIGADE MAJOR.
102nd INFANTRY BRIGADE.

Issued at 7/- to :-

G.O.C.	Copy No. 1.
Brigade Major	" " 2.
Staff Captain	" " 3.
Signals	" " 4.
Bde. Transport Officer.	" " 5.
22nd Bn. N.F.	" " 6.
23rd Bn. N.F.	" " 7.
25th Bn. N.F.	" " 8.
102 M.G.Coy.	" " 9.
102 L.T.M.B.	" " 10.
240 M.G.Coy.	" " 11.
203 Field Coy. R.E. ..	" " 12.
102nd Field Amb.	" " 13.
No.3 Coy.Div.Train	" " 14.
Brigade Supply Off.	" " 15.
Diary and File	Copies 16 & 17.
34th Division	Copy No.18.
101st Inf.Bde.	" " 19.
103rd Inf. Bde.	" " 20.
Transport Off. 20th rk	21

TABLE "A". March on FEB. 9th. 1918.

No. in order of march.	Troops	Starting Point Place	Time to pass.	ROUTE	DESTINATION.	REMARKS.
1	Bde. H.Q., Signal Section.	Brigade Headquarters.	9.0 a.m.	MERCATEL – FICHEUX – BLAIRVILLE.	Sandpit BLAIRVILLE.	Bde. H.Q. closes at N.36.c.8.0. at 9.0 a.m. Transport 20th N.F. less detached vehicles will join column at 5 cross roads immediately N. of H in MERCATEL at 9.26 a.m. and march in rear of Signal Section.
2	22nd N.F.	5 cross roads immediately N. of H in MERCATEL	9.30 am	FICHEUX – BLAIRVILLE.	No. 2 Camp BLAIRVILLE.	300X in rear of Brigade Headquarters.
3	23rd N.F.	5 cross roads immediately N. of H in MERCATEL.	9.41 am	FICHEUX – BLAIRVILLE.	No. 5 Camp BLAIRVILLE.	300X in rear of 22nd Bn. N.F.
4	25th N.F.	Railway bridge over road just N. of I in BOISLEUX ST. MARC.	10.0 am	BOISLEUX AU MONT – FICHEUX – BLAIRVILLE.	No. 4 Camp BLAIRVILLE.	After cross roads at F in FICHEUX to be 500X in rear of 23rd N.F.
5	102 L.T.M.B.	Railway bridge over road just N. of I in BOISLEUX ST. MARC.	10.10 am	BOISLEUX AU MONT – FICHEUX – BLAIRVILLE.	No. 3 Camp BLAIRVILLE.	200X in rear of 25th Bn. N.F. Bde. elementary Signal class will march with 102 L.T.M.B. under orders of O.C. 102 L.T.M.B. and will join Signal section at the Sandpit BLAIRVILLE, on arrival.
6	102 Fld.Amb.	–	–	–	–	No move. Remains at No. 1 Camp, BLAIRVILLE.
7	102 M.G.Coy.	–	–	–	No. 6 Camp BLAIRVILLE.	Under orders issued by 34th Div. Joins 102nd Bde. Group on arrival.
8	240 M.G.Coy.	–	–	–	No. 5 Camp BLAIRVILLE.	Under orders issued by 34th Div. Joins 102nd Bde. Group on arrival.
9	208 Fld.Co.	–	–	–	No. 5 Camp BLAIRVILLE.	Under orders issued by C.R.E. 34th Div. Joins 102nd Bde. Group on arrival.
10	No. 5 Div.Train	–	–	–	No. 5 Camp BLAIRVILLE.	March independently.

TABLE "B". March on Feb. 10th 1918. To accompany 102nd Bde. Order No. 190.

Serial No.	Troops in order of march	Starting Point. Place.	Time to pass.	ROUTE.	DESTINATION.	R E M A R K S.
1	Bde. H.Q., Signal Section and 1/pdr 20th N.F. (less detached vehicles).	Cross Roads BLAIRVILLE.	9.0 a.m.	BRETENCOURT - GROSVILLE - BEAUMETZ - Les-LOGES - MONCHIET.	GOUY-EN-ARTOIS	Bde. H.Q. closes at BLAIRVILLE at 8.30 a.m.
2	23rd N.F.	Cross Roads BLAIRVILLE.	9.5 a.m.	As for Bde. H.Q. to GOUY-EN-ARTOIS thence direct.	BARLY.	300ˣ in rear of Bde. H.Q.
3	25th N.F.	Cross Roads BLAIRVILLE.	9.13 a.m.	As for Bde. H.Q.	GOUY-EN-ARTOIS	300ˣ in rear of 23rd N.F.
4	22nd N.F.	Cross Roads BLAIRVILLE.	9.27 a.m.	As for Bde. H.Q.	GOUY-en-ARTOIS	300ˣ in rear of 25th N.F.
5	240 M.G. Coy.	Cross Roads BLAIRVILLE.	9.38 a.m.	As for Bde. H.Q.	MONCHIET.	300ˣ in rear of 22nd N.F.
6	102 M.G. Coy.	Cross Roads BLAIRVILLE.	9.41 a.m.	As for Bde. H.Q.	BARLY.	20ˣ in rear of 240 M.G. Coy.
7	103 L.T.M.B.	Cross Roads BLAIRVILLE.	9.44 a.m.	As for Bde. H.Q. to GOUY-en-ARTOIS thence direct.	BARLY.	20ˣ in rear of 102 M.G. Coy.
8	203rd Field Co. R.E.	Cross Roads BLAIRVILLE.	9.48 a.m.	As for Bde. H.Q. to GOUY-en-ARTOIS thence direct.	LAVINCOURT.	300ˣ in rear of 102 L.T.M.B.
9	102 Fld. Amb.	Cross Roads BLAIRVILLE.	10.3 a.m.	As for Bde. H.Q. to GOUY-en-ARTOIS thence direct.	LAVINCOURT.	20ˣ in rear of 203rd Fld. Co. R.E.
10	No. 3 Coy. Div. Train less Baggage Section.	-	-	-	GOUY-en-ARTOIS	March independently.

TABLE "C"   March on Feb. 14th 1918   To accompany 102nd Bde. Order No.130

SERIAL No.	Troops in order of march	Starting Point - Place	Starting Point - Time to pass	ROUTE	DESTINATION	R E M A R K S
1	Bde. H.Q. Signal Section. T'port 20th NF (less detached vehicles)	Stream on FOSSEUX Rd. Sn. W. of GOUY-EN-ARTOIS Church	9.a.m.	FOSSEUX - BARLY - AVESNES-LE-COMTE - GIVENCHY-LE-NOBLE	AMBRINES	Bde.H.Q. close at GOUY-EN-ARTOIS at 8.30.a.m.
2.	25th N.F.	As for Bde. H.Q.	9.5.a.m.	As for Bde. H.Q.	AMBRINES	500x in rear of Bde.H.Q.
3.	22nd N.F.	As for Bde. H.Q.	9.13.a.m.	As for Bde. H.Q. to AMBRINES thence direct	MAIZIERES	500x in rear of 25th N.F
4.	23rd N.F.	Cross Roads BARLY 200x N.W. of the Church	10.10.a.m	AVESNES-LE-COMTE - GIVENCHY-LE-NOBLE - VILLERS-SUR-SIMON	PENIN	300x in rear of 22nd N.F
5.	102 L.T.M.B	As for 23rd N.F	10.21.a.m	AVESNES-LE-COMTE - GIVENCHY-LE-NOBLE	AMBRINES	300x in rear of 23rd N.F
6.	102 M.G.Coy.	As for 23rd N.F	10.22.a.m	AVESNES-LE-COMTE - BLAVINCOURT	SARS LEZ BOIS	20x in rear of 102 L.T.M.B.
7.	240 M.G.Coy.	Junction of road & track 200x N. of IVONCHIET	9.5.a.m.	GOUY-EN-ARTOIS - FOSSEUX-BARLY - AVESNES-LE-COMTE - BLAVINCOURT	DENIER	20x in rear of 102 M.G.C
8.	208 Fld.Coy.R.E	Road Junction 200x NE of BAVINCOURT Church	9.47.a.m	BARLY-AVESNES-LE-COMTE - GIVENCHY-LE-NOBLE	VILLERS-SUR-SIMON	300x in rear of 240 M.G.C
9.	102 Fld.Amb.	As for 208 Fld.Co.R.E.	10.2.a.m.	As for 208 Fld.Co R.E.	VILLERS-SUR-SIMON	20x in rear of 208 Fld.Co.RE
10.	No.2.Coy.Div. Train				SERIENCOURT	March independently

War Diary

SECRET.

ADMINISTRATIVE INSTRUCTIONS No. 12.

The subject of this memorandum is to be kept Secret and precautions taken to prevent it falling into the hands of the enemy.

1. The Brigade will be re-organised in accordance with 34th Division No. G/193 (issued to 20th and 21st North'd. Fus. only).

2. The Order of Battle of the Brigade from 12 noon February 3rd will be :-
    22nd (S)Bn. North'd. Fus. — 3rd Tyneside Scottish.
    23rd (S)Bn. North'd. Fus. — 4th Tyneside Scottish.
    25th (S)Bn. North'd. Fus. — 2nd Tyneside Irish.

3. This will be effected by :-
    (a) Disbanding the 20th and 21st Bns. North'd. Fus.
    (b) Transferring the 25th Bn. North'd. Fus. intact from the 103rd Infantry Brigade to the 102nd Infantry Brigade.

4. Personnel of disbanded Battalions will be transferred to other Battalions of the North'd. Fus. as shown in Table "A" attached.

5. The re-organisation of the Brigade will be carried out on the following lines:-

    All deficiencies in Specialists in the Battalions about to form this Brigade (ie. 22nd, 23rd and 25th Bns. North'd. Fus.) will first be made up to Establishment.

    All drafts to these Battalions will be of full strength as laid down in Table "A".

    Preference will be given as far as possible to men who have been longest in the Tyneside Scottish Brigade to be reposted to one of the Battalions of this Brigade.

    In detailing drafts for Units not in this Brigade, men will first be selected who have previously served in those Units. The remainder will be fairly divided; N.C.Os and men being given as far as possible the choice to which Unit they will go. Except as provided for above, no picking out of good men for certain Units will be made.

6. Officers of the 20th and 21st North'd. Fus. will be reposted as in Table "B" attached.

7. Certain Specialists will be disposed of as under:-
    (a) PIPERS.- The Pipers and Drummers of the 20th North'd. Fus. will be transferred intact to the 22nd North'd. Fus. and those of the 21st North'd. Fus. to the 23rd North'd. Fus. Pipes, Drums and Pipers' Clothing and Equipment etc., will be handed over to the 22nd and 23rd North'd. Fus. respectively. A careful record of the Equipment so transferred will be made by all Battalions concerned and receipts given and taken. Os/c., 22nd and 23rd North'd. Fus. are reminded that these Pipes and certain articles of Equipment are the property of the Tyneside Scottish Committee who will be asked their wishes as to their final disposal.

    (b) Attached Men.- 8 of the men of the 20th North'd. Fus. now attached to 102nd Machine Gun Coy will be transferred to 22nd North'd. Fus. The remaining 4 men of the 20th North'd. Fus. now attached to 102nd Machine Gun Company and the 2 men now attached to 102nd Trench Mortar Battery will be transferred to 25th North'd. Fus.

(b) Attached men (Old) The 7 men of the 21st North'd. Fus now attached 260th Machine Gun Coy will be transferred to the 25th North'd. Fus.
These men will remain attached as at present on reposting.

All the men included in (a) &(b) above will be included in the numbers to be sent as drafts as shown in Table "A".

8. No personnel which is on the STRENGTH according to War Establishments of other Units such as 102nd Trench Mortar Battery and Brigade Headquarters will be transferred notwithstanding the fact that they may be on the ESTABLISHMENT of Battalions to be disbanded.

9. Reference 34th Division No. G/193 para.7, (instructions for C.Os of Battalions about to be disbanded.
All Nominal Rolls will be submitted to Divisional Headquarters "A" direct.
An amended roll of Officers and men on Leave or Courses in England will be submitted to Divisional Headquarters "A" direct shewing date on which they are expected to arrive in France and the Unit to which they have been posted.

10. Headquarters of disbanded Battalions will remain with the Division until all details connected with re-organisation are complete. They will continue to be administered by their original Brigade. They will eventually be withdrawn to the Corps Reinforcement Camp.

11. In the event of numbers to be transferred to Battalions outside the Division falling below those given in Table "A" Battalions will report to Brigade Headquarters by 12 noon on the 2nd. the Total numbers actually available to move and the numbers still on leave etc., who will rejoin later.

12. The following instructions will be followed as regards the posting of Officers and O.R. to other Battalions.

(a) Names of Officers posted to other Battalions will be reported to Brigade Headquarters who will repeat by wire to D.H.Q. Brigade Commanders will decide as to the posting of Officers.
(b) Regimental Signallers will be posted as in Table "A".
(c) Warrant Officers and N.C.Os above the rank of Sergeant will not be posted to other Battalions but will be disposed of as may be ordered by the A.G.
(d) N.C.Os of and below the rank of Sergeant will be posted in the proportion of 2 Sergeants, 3 Corporals, 3 Lance Corporals, to every 50 Privates, and 1 Lance Sergeant in addition for every 100 Other Ranks.
(e) All other personnel eg. men on leave, Specialists on Courses, etc. are to be included proportionately in the postings ordered herein.

Every endeavour is to be made to post Officers and men who have served together, to the same Unit.

13. Special attention will be paid to the maintenance of a record of all personnel of disbanded Battalions during the course of re-organisation.

14. ACCOMMODATION. - After 2 pm February 3rd the Brigade will be accommodated as follows:-

22nd North'd. Fus.	Northumberland Lines.
23rd North'd Fus.	York Lines.
25th North'd. Fus.	Durham Lines B.
102nd Trench Mortar Battery.	Durham Lines A.
Brigade Signal Class.	Durham Lines. A.

(3)

14. ACCOMMODATION – (continued)

Headquarters, 20th North'd. Fus.) No. 4. Camp BLAINVILLE.
Headquarters, 21st North'd. Fus.) (in lines vacated by
and drafts for 12/13th North'd.   ) 25th North'd. Fus.)
Fus.   )
Drafts of 21st North'd. Fus for
1st North'd. Fus.   Durham Lines B.
102nd Machine Gun Company.   MORY.

All Transport as at present.
On the 4th February the transport of the 21st and 25th North'd. Fus will change places.

15. MOVES.— The necessary moves will be carried out in accordance with Table "C".

The drafts of the 21st North'd. Fus. for the 1st Bn. North'd. Fus. will remain in Durham Lines.

16. RATIONS.— All drafts will take with them the unconsumed portion of the days rations. Rations for the following day will be adjusted by the Supply Officer as required.

17. O.C., 20th North'd. Fus. will hand over that portion DURHAM LINES A (less 6 huts reserved for 102nd Trench Mortar Battery and Brigade Signal Class) now occupied by him to O.C. 1st East Lancs Regiment by 3 pm February 3rd.

Durham Lines B will be vacated by 21st North'd. Fus. and such portions of the East Lancs as are now in it by 4pm.

The 25th North'd. Fus. on arrival about 4pm will take over Durham Lines B (less 6 huts reserved for draft of 21st North'd. Fus. for 1st North'd. Fus.)

18. All other instructions contained in 34th Division No. G/195 not mentioned in these instructions will be complied with by Officers Commanding Battalions to be disbanded.

P Brough
Lieut.
A/Staff Captain.
2/2/18.   102nd INFANTRY BRIGADE.

Table "A"

To be posted from	Off.	O.R.	No. of stragglers	To be posted to	Division	Date of move	Remarks
20th N.F.	10	220	8	24th N.F.	34	Feb. 3rd	
	10	200	-	15th N.F.	34	Feb. 3rd	
	12	250	9	22nd N.F.	34	Feb. 3rd	
	5	90	-	23rd N.F.	34	Feb. 3rd	
21st N.F.	7	150	-	23rd N.F.	34	Feb. 3rd	
	12	250	10	25th N.F.	34	Feb. 3rd	
	7	150	-	1st N.F.	3	Feb. 4th	Instructions to be issued later.
	8	175	-	12th/13th N.F.	21	Feb. 5th	By rail fro SOLEUX J. 041
To be posted to	Off.	O.R.	No. of stragglers	To be posted from	Division	Date of move	
22nd N.F.	12	250	9	20th N.F.		Feb. 3rd	
	1	50	-	26th N.F.		Feb. 3rd	
23rd N.F.	5	90	-	20th N.F.		Feb. 3rd	
	7	150	-	21st N.F.		Feb. 3rd	
	1	50	-	26th N.F.		Feb. 3rd	
	12	250	10	21st N.F.		Feb. 3rd	
	1	50	-	26th N.F.		Feb. 3rd	

TABLE "B"

Postings of Officers of 20th and 21st Bns. Northd. Fusiliers.

20th _n_ N.F.

To 9th N.F.	To 18th N.F.	To 22nd N.F.	To 23rd N.F.	To POOL
2/Lt. G.N. Borland	A/Capt. J. Johnstone	Capt. F. Nixon	Capt. A.P. Ker.	
" C.H. Walker	Lieut. N.R. Futers	2/Lt. A. Woodhead	Lieut. D.E. Ward.	
" H.G. Jamieson.	2/Lt. J. Mills	2/Lt. G.R. Lingard	Lieut. P.H.L. Brough	
" A. Hillery	2/Lt. G.R. Schooling	2/Lt. W. Wright	2/Lt. L.F. Leathard	
" V. Mason	2/Lt. J.L. Loughton, M.C.	2/Lt. G.N. Beales	2/Lt. W.T.V. Cole	
" J. Howson	2/Lt. J.J. —bler	2/Lt. C. Constable		
	2/Lt. W.L. Rough	2/Lt. A.C. Leah		
	2/Lt. G.A. Peacock	2/Lt. P.J. Baldwin		
	2/Lt. R.W. Silk	2/Lt. W. Burt		
	2/Lt. C. Logan	2/Lt. E.W. Bell		
		Lieut. H.J. Hardy		
		2/Lt. R. Wilkins		

21st N.F.

To 1st N.F.	To 12th/13th N.F.	To 23rd N.F.	To 25th N.F.	To POOL
Capt. S.A. Turnbull	Capt. A.V. Curry	Capt. S.H. Matthews	Lieut. J.K. Fraser	2/Lt. H.W. Horsel
2/Lt. J.C. Thompson	2/Lt. E.C. Jones	Capt. G.S. Pattull	2/Lt. J.H. Signey	" F.T. Davis
2/Lt. J.B. Casee	2/Lt. H.F. Dodd	Lt. L.V. Grice	2/Lt. C.J. Peckston	" J.R. Naylor
2/Lt. W. Blenkinsop	2/Lt. C. Remsay	Lt. N.B. Pigg	2/Lt. T.H. Pullein	" G.J. Dear
2/Lt. J. Richards	2/Lt. W.S. Bell	2/Lt. G.H. Graham	2/Lt. J.S. Bowmer	" J.F. Larra
			2/Lt. H. Bull	" —dale.
2/Lt. G.E. Redpath	2/Lt. T.W.T. Richardson	2/Lt. H.H. Davies	2/Lt. R.D. Potter	" J.W. Hunt
2/Lt. T. Williams	2/Lt. R.W. Mustard	2/Lt. C.J. Robson	2/Lt. W.A. Renshaw	
	2/Lt. H.J. Johnson		2/Lt. A. Arthur	
			2/Lt. J.H. Taylor	
			2/Lt. E. Calder.	
			2/Lt. D. Gallon.	

TABLE "C" - TABLE OF MOVES.

Date	Unit	Time to start	From	To	Remarks
Feb. 3rd	25th N.F. less transport	2 p.m.	BLAIRVILLE	BERLES "J" Lines	R.O. to re-arrange at under orders of 103 Bde.
Feb. 3rd	1st drafts of 20th N.F.	2 p.m.	BERLES LINES	to join new Bns.	
Feb. 3rd	Drafts of 21st N.F. for 22nd and 25th N.F.	2 p.m.	DURHAM LINES	to join new Bns.	
Feb. 3rd	H.Q. 20th N.F.	Between 2 p.m. and 4 p.m.	DURHAM LINES	No. 4 Camp BLAIRVILLE to lines vacated by 25th N.F.	Under Bn. arrangements, to report to Area Commandant, A.D.GUNN, for accommodation.
Feb. 3rd	H.Q. 21st N.F. and R. drafts for 12th/13th N.F.	Between 2 p.m. and 4 p.m.	DURHAM LINES		
Feb. 3rd	103 L.T.M.B.	2 p.m.	YORK LINES	DURHAM LINES	M.T.O. will arrange necessary transport
Feb. 3rd	Bde. Signal Class	2 p.m.	YORK LINES	DURHAM LINES	To be arranged by 103 Bde. Signals.
Feb. 4th	Transport 25th N.F.	10 a.m.	BERRED LINES	to lines vacated by 21st N.F. transport near CAULIEN LINES	
Feb. 4th	Transport 21st N.F.	10 a.m.	lines near CAULIEN LINES	No. 4 Camp BLAIRVILLE lines vacated by transport of 25th N.F.	To be attached to 21 Bde. A.S.C.
Feb. 5th	Draft of 21st N.F. for 12th/13th N.F.		BLAIRVILLE	BAISIEUX or other station	To proceed by train to 12th/13th N.F.
Feb. 4th	Draft of 21st N.F. for 1st N.F.				Instructions will be issued later.

TS 67/9E

Appendix 2 will be issued later.

SECRET

T.S. 67/98   Copy No. 2

Preparatory orders for move by train

while in G.H.Q. reserve.

Ref. Map
Sheet
LENS.

19 : 2 : 18

1.   During the time that 34th Division is in G.H.Q. reserve all units must be prepared to move at short notice.

2.   Moves that may be ordered, will probably be either by strategical or tactical trains.
       It is possible that the first unit of 102nd Brigade Group to entrain may be required to do so 8 hours after issue of orders.

3.   In the event of a move by strategical train units will be conveyed complete with all transport from ST.POL Station. For detailed instructions see Appendix 1. Each unit, on receipt of this letter, will send an Officer to reconnoitre the route to St POL Station as laid down in Table A attached, and the watering and forming up places there.

4.   In the event of a move by tactical train a portion only of transport will accompany units on the trains, the remainder proceeding by march route under orders of O.C. No. 3 Coy. Div. Train. The entraining stations in this case are not known yet. For detailed instructions see Appendix 2.

5.   The following instructions will be adhered to in the event of a move either by strategical or tactical train. :-

(a)   All heavy baggage, packs and surplus blankets (see sub-para. (b) below) will be stacked in stores under unit arrangements. Stores for this purpose will be selected at once and their position reported to Brigade Headquarters. A guard will be detailed for each store by the unit concerned and will be provided with 5 days rations.
       This heavy baggage, etc. is eventually to be moved by lorries under Divisional arrangements. The guards will then act as loading parties.

(b)   Dress will be "Fighting Order" as laid down in S.S. 135 (Jan. 1918) except that no extra S.A.A., bombs, flares or sandbags will be carried on the men.
       Greatcoats and one blanket per man will be carried on the men.

(c)   Each unit will send a cyclist orderly to report to the Staff Captain at the entraining station two hours before the time of departure of the train on which they are to travel.

(d)   Men will entrain with water bottles full.
       Water carts will entrain full.
       Feeds for all animals entrained will be carried on the train.
       Units must provide breast and head ropes to secure animals in the trucks.
       Camp kettles will be taken in the trucks with the men.

/ (e) Units will

5.. (contd.)

(e) Units will make every endeavour to leave their billets in a clean and sanitary condition.
Area stores will be handed over to Billet Wardens if possible or left with heavy baggage.
Units will, if possible, obtain from the Mayors of the villages in which they are billetted, a statement of any claims for damage. Such claims as are admitted will be counter-signed and returned to the Mayor.

(f) Attention is called to Field Service Regulations, Part I, Sections 34 to 39 inclusive.

ACKNOWLEDGE.

Major.
BRIGADE MAJOR.
102nd INFANTRY BRIGADE.

Distribution -

```
                G.O.C. ................    Copy No.  1
                Brigade Major  ........      "   "   2
                Staff Captain  ........      "   "   3
                Brigade Transport Officer    "   "   4
                Signals .............        "   "   5
                Transport 20th N.F. ...      "   "   6
                          22nd  *    ...     "   "   7
                          23rd  *    ....    "   "   8
                          25th  *    ...     "   "   9

                102nd L. G. Coy .......      "   "  10
                102nd L.T.M.B. ........      "   "  11
                208th Field Co. R.E. ..      "   "  12
                No. 3 Coy. Div. Train ..     "   "  13
                102nd Field Ambulance ..     "   "  14
                240th L. G. Coy. .....       "   "  15
                231st Div. Employ. Co...     "   "  16
                H.Q. R.A. ............       "   "  17
                H.Q. 34th Div ........       "   "  18  ) for
                R.T.O. St POL ........       "   "  19  ) information.
                --
                Diary and File ........    Copies  20 and 21
                --
                Spare .......... (3 copies) .. 22, 23 and 24.
```

APPENDIX 1

Instructions for move by Strategical Train.
----

1. Units will march to ST.POL Station and entrain there in accordance with Table A attached.

2. Transport will arrive at ST.POL Station 3 hours, and dismounted personnel 1½ hours before the time of departure of the train.

   Entrainment must be completed ½ hour before the time of departure of the train.

3. On arrival at ST.POL Station all troops will form up in the station yard. An Officer will be sent ahead to ascertain from the R.T.O. whether the troops may enter the station and the portion of the yard allotted them to form up.
   No troops are to enter the station until permission to do so has been obtained from the R.T.O.
   Animals will be watered and any mens' water bottles that require it, filled.

4. Each unit will hand to the R.T.O. at ST.POL Station ½ hour before any portion of the unit arrives, an accurate state showing the numbers of Officers, O.R., Animals and Vehicles to proceed by the train. A duplicate copy will be handed to the Staff Captain.

   Detached Companies (see Table A) will furnish similar states.

5. Each unit will hand to the Staff Captain at the Entraining Station a state showing the number of Officers, O.R. and Animals left behind.

6. 25th N.F. will detail 1 Company with a Field Cooker and team to report to the R.T.O. ST POL 4 hours before the time of departure of the first train to act as loading party for all trains, except train No. 21, for the Brigade Group.

   The R.T.O. will allot billets for this Company on application. Rations will be arranged by O.C. 25th N.F.

7. 208th Field Co. R.E. will be responsible for loading train No. 21. The whole Company will be at the entraining Station 3 hours before the time of departure of this train.

8. The Company 22nd N.F. travelling on the first train will act as unloading party at the Detraining Station for the whole Brigade Group. The R.T.O. at the Detraining Station will allot billets.

9. Loading and unloading parties will work under the orders of R.T.O's concerned.

   The loading party at ST POL will travel on Train No. 18 to rejoin its unit; the unloading party at the detraining station will rejoin its unit on completion of work.

10. Advance parties as under will proceed on the first train -

    Bde. H.Q. .... 1 Off. (*)   1 N.C.O.
    Each Infy. Battn. ..... 1 Off.   5 O.R.
    M.G. Coy. & Field Co.R.E. 1 Off.   1 O.R.
    Other units .... 1 Off. or   1 O.R.
              (*) In Command of whole party.
    They will march independently to ST POL Station and report to the Staff Captain there.

11.   Baggage wagons will be sent to units as soon as orders to entrain are issued. They will march to the station and entrain with units.

Supply wagons will travel loaded and accompany units. Unless otherwise ordered these wagons will proceed to Group Refilling point, A.BRINES, pick up 1 days rations, join units and march with them to the station.

12.   Transport 20th N.F. will pick up 1 days rations at Group Refilling point and remain in present billets until orders are received from Div. H.Q. as to its disposal. The Transport Officers may receive orders in this connection from an Officer of Div. Staff at FR.V NT Station.

TABLE A - Entrainment by Strategical Train.

Serial No. of Train.	Entraining Station.	Date	Time of departure.	Route to Entraining Station.	Composition.	Detraining station	Destination.
3	ST POL			MAIZIERES, FOUFFLIN, RICAMETZ, ROELLECOURT.	102 Bde. H.Q., 102 Bde. Sig. Section, 102 M.G.Co. 102 L.T.M.B., 1 Coy., 1 Cooker and team 2nd R.W., billetting parties.		
6	ST POL			FOUFFLIN, RICAMETZ, ROELLECOURT.	22nd N.F. less 1 Coy. 1 Cooker and team.		
9	ST POL			MAIZIERES, FOUFFLIN, RICAMETZ, ROELLECOURT.	23rd N.F. less 1 Coy. 1 Cooker and team.		
12	ST POL			MAIZIERES, FOUFFLIN, RICAMETZ, ROELLECOURT.	25th N.F. less 1 Coy. 1 Cooker and team.		
15	ST POL			DENIER, AMBRINES, MAIZIERES, FOUFFLIN, RICAMETZ, ROELLECOURT.	240th M.G. Coy., D.H.Co. 1 Coy., 1 Cooker and team, 23rd N.F. H.Q. R.E.		
18	ST POL			AMBRINES, MAIZIERES, FOUFFLIN, RICAMETZ, ROELLECOURT.	1 Coy. 1 Cooker and team 25th N.F., 102 Field Ambulance.		
21	ST POL			AMBRINES, MAIZIERES, FOUFFLIN, RICAMETZ, ROELLECOURT.	No. 3 Coy. Train, 208th Field Co. R.E.		

The time of departure of the first train and the interval of time between trains will be notified when received. Units will act in accordance with the above table on receipt of this notification. Intervals of time between trains will probably be 3 hours.

To accompany T.S. 67/98

APPENDIX 2.
Move by Tactical Train.

1. The 102nd Brigade Group will entrain in accordance with the attached Table B.

2. The trains available for the Group will probably consist of 2 coaching stock trains and 2 omnibus type trains.

3. No vehicles or horses can be conveyed on coaching stock trains. No G.S. wagons may be carried on omnibus type trains used for "Tactical Trains".

4. All transport not detailed in Table B will proceed by road under orders of O.C. No. 3 Coy. Div. Train. Assembly points for transport will be notified when orders for entrainment are issued.

5. Troops to entrain in coaching stock trains will arrive at the entraining station 1 hour before the time of departure of the train.

6. Transport and loading parties for omnibus type trains will arrive at the station 3 hours before the time of departure of the train. The loading party for the first omnibus type train will be 100 men 208th Field Co. R.E., that for the second train 100 men 102nd Machine Gun Company.

7. Each unit will hand to the R.T.O. at the entraining station ½ hour before any portion of the unit arrives, a state showing the numbers of Officers, O.R., animals and vehicles, to proceed by the train.
A duplicate copy and a state showing the numbers of Officers, O.R., animals and vehicles left behind, will be handed to the Staff Captain at the entraining station.

8. The unexpended portion of the days ration and the next days ration will be taken by units on the train. In the latter case the rations will be taken under arrangements to be made by O.C. No. 3 Bo. Div. Train to the entraining station and loaded on the omnibus type train of the unit concerned.

9. Officers in excess of 30 per battalion will march with that portion of their units transport proceeding by road.

Acknowledge.

[signature]
Major.
BRIGADE MAJOR.
102nd INFANTRY BRIGADE.

Distribution — As for "Preparatory orders for move by train while in G.H.Q. reserve." less H.Q. R.A. and R.T.O. St. POL.
and 231st DEC

Table B. — Entrainment by Tactical Train.

Serial No.	Date	Time	Entraining Station	Route to Entraining Station	Description of train	Composition	Detraining Station	Destination
					First Train. Coaching Stock. 2 Brake Vans 2 1st Class Coaches 2 Covered Waggons 44 Trucks	Dismounted portion of Bde. H.Q 22nd N.F. 23rd N.F. with Lewis Guns. 35th N.F. with Lewis Guns. 240 M.G.C. dismounted personnel		
					Second Train Coaching Stock --ditto--			
					First Train. Omnibus Type 1 Passenger Coach 30 Covered Waggons 17 Flat Trucks 2 Brake Vans	Proportion of Div. H.Q. Mounted portion of Bde. H.Q. 1 L.Gs. Waggon for cooks. Bde. Signal Section, including attd. with transport. 4 L.Gs. Waggons for) Lewis Guns.) 1 L.Gs. Waggon for) for S.A.A.) Battn. 2 Water Carts 2 Cookers 1 Mess Cart 11 Chargers 7 Pack Animals Maltes Cart with medical personnel Field Co.R.E. with 1 L.Gs Waggon		
					Second Train Omnibus Type --ditto--	102 M.G.C. with transport up to 240 M.G.C. " " 22 Axles. Field Amb. with 2 L.Gs. Waggons 2 L.Gs.Waggons for tools for Bn. L.T.M.Bty. with mortars		

War Diary.   Copy No 14

ADMINISTRATIVE INSTRUCTIONS No. 13.

Reference 54th Division Administrative Instructions No. 34..
(issued to Battalions and Bde..Transport Officer only),
and 102nd Infantry Brigade Operation Order No. 190.

1. **EXTRA TRANSPORT.**

    The transport of the 20th North'd. Fus. will be allotted as follows for the conveyance of blankets and heavy baggage.

22nd, 23rd, 25th Bns. North'd. Fus.	each 2 limbered G.S.Wagons.
102nd & 240th M.G.Coys, 208th F.Coy R.E.	each 1 Field Kitchen with 1 Cook.
102nd T.M.Battery.	2 G.S.Wagons 1 Water Cart
H.Q., 20th North'd. Fus.	4 Riders, 1 Maltese Cart.
H.Q., 21st North'd. Fus.	4 Riders.
Billeting Party.	2 limbered G.S.Wagons.
Bde. Headquarters.	Remainder.

    This transport will report at Headquarters of Units at 7am February 9th, except the Field Kitchens for 102nd and 240th M.G.Coys and 208th F.Coy R.E. which will join these Units on arrival in Camp at BLAIREVILLE. They will march to BLAIREVILLE with Brigade Headquarters.

    All detached vehicles of 20th North'd. Fus transport will rejoin Brigade Headquarters at AMERINES by 6pm February 11th.

    Transport personnel and Cooks will be rationed by Units to which they are attached, for consumption on 10th and 11th February.

    Os/c., 22nd, 23rd and 25th North'd. Fus will each detail one Cook accustomed to Field Kitchens to report to Transport Officer 20th North'd. Fus. on the 8th instant bringing rations for the 9th; they will be returned by 6pm on the 11th instant.

2. **TRANSPORT.**

    Os/c., Units are responsible that their Transport Vehicles are not overloaded.

3. **LORRIES.**

    Lorries from the 18th D.S.C. are reporting as detailed in Table "A" attached at 7-30am 9th February for the conveyance of blankets and heavy baggage. They will remain with the Unit to which they are allotted throughout the move, rejoining the D.S.C. on the evening of February 11th. When necessary they may do two journeys a day but not more.

    Infantry Battalions will detail an Officer, other Units an Officer or N.C.O. to take charge of the lorries and remain with them throughout the move.

4. **BILLETING PARTIES** will be detailed as under:-

	Off.	O.R.
Brigade Headquarters	1	1
Each Infantry Battalion.	1	5
102nd M.G.Coy.	1	1
240th M.G.Coy.	1	1
208th F.Coy. R.E.	1	1
102nd Field Ambulance.	-	1
102nd T.M.Battery.	-	1
No. 3 Coy. Train.	-	1

    2/Lt. H.H.DAVIES, M.C. 23rd North'd. Fus. will Command the Billeting Parties and make all arrangements for their moves etc. All parties will report to him in the first instance at the Area Commandants Office, HENDECOURT at 9am February 9th.

    All Officers and other ranks will be provided with bicycles or horses.

    The Interpreters attached to Brigade Headqrs., will accompany the party.

    All Billeting Parties will bring rations for 3 days.

(1)

(2)

4. **BILLETING PARTIES** - continued.

A limbered G.S. Wagon from transport 20th North'd. Fus. will report at ROMAN LINES and one at YORK and NORTHUMBERLAND LINES at 7-30am February 9th to collect blankets and kits of Billeting parties from Units in those camps.

These wagons will proceed independently to Brigade Headquarters BLAIRVILLE.

Parties from all other Units must make their own arrangements for conveying blankets and kits to Brigade Headquarters (BLAIRVILLE) by 9am February 9th.

5. **BILLETS.**

All O.C/s., Units will ensure that billets are left absolutely clean. Rear Parties will be left behind if necessary. Where possible certificates will be obtained from Area Commandants to the effect that there are no complaints in this respect.

6. **AREA STORES.**

All Area Stores (vide Third Army Routine Order 1428) in the present Area will be handed over to the Camp Commandants concerned and receipts obtained.

7. **MOVE OF H.Q. 20th and 21st North'd. Fus.**

The lorry detailed for the H.Q. of 20th and 21st North'd. Fus. will convey all baggage of these two Headquarters direct to their destination GRAND RULLECOURT. It may also carry the rifles, packs and ammunition of the H.Q. personnel. Each of these H.Q. will send two men with the lorry, all other personnel proceeding by March Route direct to GRAND RULLECOURT on the 9th instant.

There are no restrictions as to route.

8. **MEDICAL ARRANGEMENTS.**

On February 9th, Sick for Evacuation will be collected by 102nd Field Ambulance before 9am.

On the 10th and 11th February Os/c., Units will notify 102nd Field Ambulance by 7-30am of the number of sick (if any) to be collected.

P Brough
Lieut.
A/STAFF CAPTAIN.
102nd INFANTRY BRIGADE.

7/2/18.

DISTRIBUTION.:-

G.O.C.	Copy No.	1.
Brigade Major.	"	2.
Staff Captain.	"	3.
Signals.	"	4.
Bde. Transport Officer.	"	5.
T.O. 20th North'd. Fus.	"	6.
22nd North'd. Fus.	"	7.
23rd North'd. Fus.	"	8.
26th North'd. Fus.	"	9.
102nd M.G. Coy.	"	10.
102nd T.M. Battery.	"	11.
249th F.C. Coy.	"	12.
208th F.Coy., R.E.	"	13.
102nd Field Ambulance.	"	14.
H.Q., 20th North'd. Fus.	"	15.
H.Q., 21st North'd. Fus.	"	16.
Diary and File.	"	17 & 18.
34th Division.	"	19.

TABLE "A" - ALLOTMENT OF LORRIES.

UNIT.	No. of lorries.	Place of reporting.	REMARKS.
Bde. H.Q.	1.	Bde. H.Q. M.28.c.8.5.	
22nd N.F.) 23rd NF.) 25th N.F.)	2 each.	-do-	Each Bn. will send a guide to be at the rendezvous at 7-50am.
H.Q. 20th N.F.) H.Q. 21st N.F.)	1.	-do-	O.C., 21st N.F. will send a guide to be at the rendezvous at 7-50am. This lorry will report at brigade H.Q. BLAIREVILLE on evening of 9th aft'r completion of work. This lorry will make 1 journey only.
102nd M.G.Coy.	1.	MORY, B.21.a.97.	This lorry will make 1 journey only.
240th M.G.Coy.	1.	Bomb Store, NEUVILLE VITASSE.	A guide from 240th M.G.Coy will be sent to be at rendezvous at 7-50am.
208th F. Coy. R.E.	1.	MORY, B.28.a.46.	

DISPOSITION·REPORTS·

SECRET   T.S. 21/53

Headquarters,
   34th Division.

DISPOSITION REPORT

BRIGADE HEADQUARTERS	GOUY-en-ARTOIS - P.18.d.7.0. Sheet 51.C.
H.Q. 20th Bn. N.F.	GRAND RULLECOURT.
H.Q. 21st Bn. N.F.	GRAND RULLECOURT.
H.Q. 22nd Bn. N.F.	GOUY-en-ARTOIS.
H.Q. 23rd Bn. N.F.	BARLY.
H.Q. 25th Bn. N.F.	GOUY-en-ARTOIS.
102nd L.T.M.B.	BARLY.
102nd M.G. Coy	BARLY.
240th M.G. Coy	MONCHIET.
208th Field Co. R.E.	BAVINCOURT.
102nd Field Ambulance	BAVINCOURT.
No. 3 Coy. Div. Train	GOUY-en-ARTOIS.

Dispositions after march to-morrow, Feb. 11th.

BRIGADE HEADQUARTERS	AMBRINES.
H.Q. 20th Bn. N.F.	GRAND RULLECOURT.
H.Q. 21st Bn. N.F.	GRAND RULLECOURT.
22nd Bn. N.F.	MAIZIERES.
23rd Bn. N.F.	PENIN.
25th Bn. N.F.	AMBRINES.
102nd L.T.M.B.	AMBRINES.
102nd M.G. Coy	SARS LEZ BOIS.
240th M.G. Coy	DENIER.
208th Field Co. R.E.	VILLERS SIR SIMON.
102nd Field Ambulance	VILLERS SIR SIMON.
No. 3 Coy. Div. Train	BERLENCOURT.

for BRIGADIER-GENERAL.
COMDG: 102nd INFANTRY BRIGADE.

10 : 2 : 1918.

SECRET   War DIARY   T.S. 21/52

Headquarters,
34th Division.

102 BRIGADE GROUP

Dispositions after march tomorrow, Feb. 9th.

102 Brigade Headquarters	.....	Sandpit, BLAIREVILLE.
22nd North'd. Fusiliers	.....	No. 2 Camp, BLAIREVILLE.
23rd North'd. Fusiliers	.....	No. 3 Camp, "
25th North'd. Fusiliers	.....	No. 4 Camp, "
102nd Machine Gun Coy	.....	No. 6 Camp, "
102nd L. T. M. Bty	.....	No. 6 Camp, "
240th Machine Gun Coy	.....	No. 5 Camp, "
208th Field Co. R.E.	.....	No. 5 Camp, "
No. 3 Coy. Div. Train	.....	No. 5 Camp, "
102nd Field Ambulance	.....	No. 1 Camp, "

***

102 B.H.Q.
8 : 2 : 18.

for BRIGADIER-GENERAL.
COMDG: 102nd INFANTRY BRIGADE.

SECRET.   T.S.21/46.

To:- Headquarters,
        34th Division.

DISPOSITIONS AFTER MOVES TO-DAY.

BRIGADE HEADQUARTERS .... M.36.c.8.0.

HQ 20th Bn. Northd. Fusiliers ...... No.4 Camp, HENDECOURT.

HQ 21st Bn. Northd. Fusiliers ...... No.4 Camp, HENDECOURT.

22nd Bn. Northd. Fusiliers ...... NORTHUMBERLAND LINES.

23rd Bn. Northd. Fusiliers ...... YORK LINES.

25th Bn. Northd. Fusiliers ...... DURHAM LINES 'B'.

102 Machine Gun Company .... Attached 40th Division.

102 Light T.M. Battery .... DURHAM LINES 'A'.

102 B.H.Q.,
3: 2: 1918.

for BRIGADIER GENERAL,
COMMDG. 102ND INFANTRY BRIGADE.

www.ingramcontent.com/pod-product-compliance
Lightning Source LLC
Chambersburg PA
CBHW081539160426
43191CB00011B/1798